Dog Vacations

Written by Carolyn West Meyer

Editing and Photos by Kel Pickens

Cover and Illustrations by Audrey Little

To Kel – truly the better half of me

Table of Contents

Trip 1   The Fall Foliage Tour of the Northeast Kingdom

Trip 2   Westward Ho!

Trip 3   Don't Mess with Texas!

Trip 4   Return to Sedona

INTRODUCTION

Just as bicycling through an area instead of driving it launches you into a new dimension, so does traveling with dogs, visiting some places you wouldn't ordinarily go had they not been on the trip. Maybe this book will inspire those with their own dogs to take them along the next time the wanderlust nudges. Our travels would never have had the depth of fun, humor, joy, or adventure if we had not taken our furry girls to share in them. Those canine bundles of love, affection, patience, spontaneity, and loyalty gave us everything they had and took only a pittance in return.

Trips are like old friends - some treat you better than others and cause you less stress. None are perfect, but some come very close to being so carefree that they seem near perfection. Others cause little annoyances almost daily, but later, sometimes much later, we can laugh about the ups and downs as we put those into perspective and see the humor in what happened. I treasure all my dog vacations and remember each one with such fondness, just like I treasure each friend and animal I've known throughout my life.

Precious memories surface at times to touch my heart. Leafing through photos that were taken so carefully on each trip placed in scrapbooks or watching videos my husband, Kel, filmed help to refresh and aid me in distinguishing each journey from the others as they tend to run together, especially when we went back to the same places several times. But even then, the circumstances were never the same. Some locations required return visits to exhaust all the rich possibilities they offered.

Without my journals to use as my skeleton there would've been no book to flesh out. Each trip was completely individual in what took place, how it made me feel, and its overall personality. I cherish them on their own merits and remember the best and worst so tenderly and poignantly. They've been given new life in this book for everyone, be they dog owners or not, to be entertained as we were with the highs and lows.

Reading these true stories, you'll share a magical time when we roamed through deep forests, contemplated the vastness of the desert, were rejuvenated by the snow-capped mountain air, or took a refreshing dip in the lake with our four-legged best friends by our sides. Even the ordinary, daily routines were enhanced by Bea's and B.B.'s presence, and the extraordinary times went far beyond what we'd imagined just as some of the dog-friendly places we discovered. So, travel along with our "pack," heading way up into the Northeast Kingdom, down south to Padre Island, to the heights of San Francisco, and the multitude of large cities, small towns, and tiny villages we explored as we mined the gold of that special bond between humans and dogs

PREFACE

Dogs have been my passion for nearly four decades. I was raised around cats, so I was a cat person growing up, never bonding with the one and only dog we had when I was still in elementary school. But after I met Kel, my second husband, I became a dog lover. I'd never really been able to relate well to dogs until he educated me about the canine brain and how it worked. He also demonstrated how you could work that canine brain to teach the dog to behave and do what you wanted him/her to do. His unorthodox training was individual to him and each different dog, but it certainly worked! I still love cats, but they've taken a backseat to the dogs Kel and I have had over our nearly forty years together.

Thinking of ourselves as a "pack," we had three large dogs spanning two decades. Jade was a Doberman, Labrador, and German shepherd mix who had the most beautiful green eyes the color of jade, therefore her name. Kel called them "pie eyes" because they were so large and round. When we first saw her, she cautiously peered out at us from under a bed as a little shy, sweet puppy with her big pie eyes. The last one left in the litter that spring, we immediately fell in love with her and had to take her home with us.

Her pup, Rapport, was a mix of seven big breeds! He was Jade's three plus his father, Bear's, four large breeds which were Great Pyrenees, Great Dane, Siberian Husky, and Newfoundland. Rapport was a true gentle giant. In all the years we had our gentle eighty pound "Orca," which was one of his many nicknames, I only heard him bark three times, and he never hurt anyone or anything. Rapport, like Jade, was black with tan markings. They looked like twins to people who didn't know them. We also referred to him as "The Clown" sometimes since he was always doing funny things that made us laugh. Also nicknamed "Rapporpoise," he made high squeaky porpoise sounds at times. That was certainly funny coming from a dog his size! He had lots of nicknames as did all of our dogs. "Baby Jade Sweetface," one of her nicknames, was a wonderful, loving mother to Rapport. We also called her "The Queen" because she pretty much ruled the roost and was dominant over her son even though he outweighed her by about thirty

7

pounds.

Rounding out our pack was Kyotee whom we found as a puppy sitting by the highway on Memorial weekend in 1987. He was half coyote and probably half Anatolian shepherd. Witnessing his coyote mother run off into the tall weeds when we stopped to save him, he tried to follow her across the busy highway. Due to his size at maturity and the coloring of his features we guessed that his daddy was an Anatolian shepherd. Coyote females sometimes bred with domesticated dogs, so we surmised that his daddy had probably taken advantage of that with the trade-off possibly being his life. He might have been dinner for the rest of the coyote pack after the mating. Kyotee turned out to be an extremely handsome dog, but he didn't start out that way. When we found him his ears and head were full of ticks and he was nearly dead from starvation. It was lucky we came along when we did, or he probably wouldn't have survived. When I finally pulled all the ticks out of him his head was as smooth as Sweet Pea's in the old Popeye cartoons. I began to call him Sweet Pea, and that nickname stuck with him for the rest of his life. He became Rapport's puppy, but he was the opposite of his "brother." Kyotee had a wild streak in him that he inherited from his mother and would try to kill any small animals that he came in contact with. We had to be very careful with him.

There was a feline member of this pack who, besides Jade and Rapport, was the exception to Kyotee's killing instinct. Yella Fella had been there even before Kel, so he had seniority. Kyotee quickly learned when he was still a puppy that this particular cat was part of the pack. He accepted him, but we still had to keep a close eye on our half coyote when he was around

8

Yella Fella, thinking he might just take a stab at him if we weren't looking.

Yella Fella, who was technically a light red color but looked yellow to me, had been born in our basement on May 18, 1978. His mother was a pregnant stray cat who'd been hanging around our house that spring. Early that morning I heard a chorus of soft mewing coming from the basement. When I went down to see what was making that sound, I found Mama Cat and her four newborn kittens. She'd gotten in through an open-air vent. Yella's mother and the other kittens were brown tabbies but he, being the only yellow one, was distinctive. I named him Yella Fella the first minute I saw him, then kept him, and found homes for the others. He was fussy and pristine, kept himself fastidiously clean, and was rather aloof to the point of snobbish. I lovingly dubbed him the Tony Randall of Cats. Our three large dogs accompanied us on numerous short day-long drives over to stay in cottages in Eureka Springs, Arkansas. Once we even took the entire pack there. But that didn't work out very well since Yella Fella found a way to escape from the cottage where we were staying. Fearing we'd never see him again after searching all over the area and even checking at the animal shelter to see if he'd been turned in, we were resigning ourselves to losing him when he decided to grace us with his presence and come back over to the house. He strolled out from some bushes across the street and over to us at the guest house in his effete way as if he were saying, "What's all the hubbub about? I'm right here, and it's time for my supper!"

Kel surmised," He's probably been watching us searching frantically while he was sitting hidden in those bushes close by. He's most likely been laughing at us while we looked for him."

I could just imagine him doing that! Relieved and happy to see him, we decided not to take him on any more trips after that.

It truly was a pack! A preening line in pecking order stretched across the living room floor. Jade would groom Rapport while Rapport worked on Kyotee. Yella Fella, being the pristine cat that he was, never took part in what to him was a disgusting activity.

It had been five years since we had a puppy, but this little girl stole my heart that fall evening, and never intending to have four dogs at the same time, we couldn't resist adding her to our pack.

Bea, whose full name that I gave her the night we first laid eyes on her, was Baby Cakes. She was a Shar Pei German shepherd mix. I'd seen her that cool November night in 1992 at our Animal Control shelter in Stillwater when she was only sixteen weeks old. She was the color of a beautiful, bright orange pumpkin with a white chest and white at the tip end of her tail. She had the most expressive face with big brown eyes and stand-up ears. She didn't have the wrinkles so characteristic of the Shar Pei breed but if you took your hands and squeezed the sides of her face together gently, she looked very much like a wrinkled Shar Pei. She quite often would have a worried look on her face even when there was nothing to worry about. She was a very gentle, sweet dog who held a baby bunny in her mouth one time as she came running over to show it to us! She was being very careful so as not to injure it by keeping her mouth slightly open while it sat inside on her tongue in the bottom of her mouth. She let Kel remove it and send it on its way. We guessed she was just trying to figure out what she should do with it. Her gentle nature

10

earned her the nickname of "Sweetness." We had numerous rabbits in our neighborhood so every time we saw one, we'd say, "There's Bea's bunny!" As she grew older, she sometimes had such a shit-eating grin on her face that she looked very clownish and made us laugh out loud. We never regretted adding her to our pack. We soon began calling her B. C. which later changed to Bea for short. Eventually, when she got older, we lovingly called her Miss Bea. She had many other nicknames as well.

By the time we got B. B. in the spring of 2000 the original pack had shrunk to just Kyotee and Bea. B.B.'s full name that I gave her was Black Bea because when I first saw her she looked just like the black version of Miss Bea, and we were told by the Animal Welfare officer that she was a Shar Pei, German shepherd mix too. She was black with a little white diamond on her chest. Her back had very coarse black fur down the middle while her sides were a bit lighter shade of blackish-gray and extremely soft like a bunny's. We thought of her as "two-toned." Like Miss Bea she had stand-up pointed ears and little round black eyes, but her snout was shorter, and she had white toes on her two back feet. Unlike Bea, she had a curly tail that would curl up even more when she was around another dog. We brought her home just as a foster dog from the Humane Society of Stillwater where Kel worked as their director. Kel had saved her life when her time ran out at Animal Welfare, and since she'd been waiting for a new home for quite some time, we wanted to give her a little break from kennel life. I figured out right away why she hadn't been adopted over all that months. She could run like she was a bullet shot out of a gun! When someone took her out for a walk on a short leash, she would let out all

11

her pent-up energy, dragging the person across the large exercise yard. She was very strong and pulled quite hard making many people shy away from adopting her after SHE walked them! I compared it to skiing behind a boat and called it dog skiing. I had done dog skiing in the past when walking Rapport and Kyotee at the same time. Once we got her home, we could never part with her.

Full grown when we got her, we never really knew how old Black Bea was, but guessed she probably was four when we fostered her, which was four years younger than Bea. She fit right into our family with Miss Bea and Kyotee, and eventually had even more nicknames than Miss Bea. One of the first ones was "Little Sprite" because she had so much energy and never seemed to age. I also said B.B. stood for "Black Beauty" because she was so beautiful to me. In her younger days, B.B. was not the gentle soul that Bea was since she was always wanting to chase rabbits. One evening when we were walking both of our dogs in our neighborhood, I decided to let B.B. off her leash so she could run free on our dead-end street. She took off like a rocket and chased a rabbit where she promptly trapped it against our fence and killed it. We were very sorry about that, but knew it was her instinct controlling her. I was really more to blame than she, so we didn't scold her for it. After all, I was the one who let her off the leash; she was just doing what came naturally.

Then on my fifty-third birthday, Sunday, December 11, 2005, we were out decorating the trees and bushes for Christmas by stringing lights in our front yard. Bea and B.B. were out loose with us. B.B. kept running around a large cedar tree near the street. We thought she might be chasing a rabbit around the tree but wouldn't be able to trap it and kill it since rabbits used the cedars to escape such encounters. She was so intent on catching the creature that she ran right into a low branch of that cedar tree and impaled herself! She dashed straight to me in pain with that broken piece of branch remaining deep in her chest next to her right shoulder like a spear. Seeing that branch sticking out and the terrified look on her face scared me more than anything ever had! Fearing this would be the end of her, we quickly put Bea in the house and loaded B.B. into the car to get to the vet clinic that we knew was open even on Sundays. We were so lucky that she hadn't hit any major arteries or veins, or we would've never been able to get her there alive since the clinic was all the way across town from where we live. It made for a very long trip since we had to leave that branch in her. We were afraid to remove it, worrying that if we did, she'd bleed to death. Thankfully, the vet did such a perfect job on her wound that you couldn't even tell where she'd been injured once it healed completely. But it was a very sad birthday for me since I was filled with dread until we got her back home the next day. Needless to say, we learned a valuable lesson and were much more careful with her from then on paying more attention when we let her run loose.

Another passion of mine is autumn. It has always been my favorite season with a new school year starting that brings excitement and expectations. For me the new year didn't start in January, it began with the new school term. That brought the football games which thrilled me even if I don't attend them anymore. It's a rather strange comfort to me just knowing that they are being played in the stadiums across town.

13

I especially love October and have such fond memories of that fall month because my parents' birthdays were in the middle of it and we always celebrated them together. My mother spoke about how much she looked forward to the "bright, blue weather of October." That's when the trees in Oklahoma begin to turn, and seeing their leaves adorned in bright oranges, reds, and yellows with flocks of geese overhead flying south for the winter and honking to each other give me butterflies of anticipation in my stomach.

The welcome crispness in the air makes me feel more alive after a hot, sweltering Oklahoma summer. It's that time you put away your summer clothes and pull out the warm sweaters and jeans that have waited patiently in their drawers or closets since they were put way in the early spring.

Of course, Halloween, my favorite holiday, makes October even more fun with all the decorations I put up each year and the scary stories and songs that I recall from my teaching and my own childhood. October is the most beautiful month in Oklahoma, and many of my friends who are bred-and-born Okies agree. Of course, I don't wait for October to arrive before I begin decorating the house, yard, and mailbox in an autumn theme. Like a pot about to boil over, I wait until the equinox takes place around the twenty-first of September to dig out the raggedy scarecrows along with some pumpkins, mums, and gourds to carefully place by our driveway and twirl a garland of golden, red, and orange leaves around the mailbox. Then on the first day of October I add spooky decorations to the display. All too soon Halloween is over, and it is a mad dash into Thanksgiving and my birthday which occurs in the very late fall. It's always a bit sad to bid goodbye to the most beautiful exhilarating season of all as my least favorite, winter, comes knocking at the door.

But the fall of 2004 was different than any I'd ever experienced before. There were no anxiety nightmares about being late to teach class on the first day of school or panic in dreams about standing up in front of my first class of the day realizing that I'd forgotten to put on my pants. Every August before school began, I would experience at least one of those. I had no worries about the principal coming to see me on that first workday in my classroom, saying, "I hate to tell you this but we're going to have to take your music room this year to use it for a regular class due to the larger enrollment."

That meant I would have to travel room-to-room with a cart and teach music in each different self-contained classroom - a very difficult thing to do. That had happened more than I liked to remember. No, none of that would ever happen to me again. I was a free woman! After teaching elementary music for twenty-nine years I was able to retire comfortably. I'd enjoyed inspiring a multitude of children to love learning music over those years, but now I was ready for a new kind of life. Now I could be more carefree with the time to travel to places I'd only dreamed about going. There were no time limits to stop me from visiting them.

I'd always wanted to see the fall foliage up in the New England states and be a "leaf peeper," as the New Englanders nicknamed the tourists who came to see the beauty of their countryside. My husband, Kel, was agreeable, so we decided to take our two dogs, Bea and B.B., with us on this road trip - our first long distance journey with them which we dubbed a "Dog Vacation."

15

Trip 1   The Fall Foliage Tour of the Northeast Kingdom

Chapter 1   B.B. Discovers Cows

"Car-Car!" I sang out excitedly setting into motion our dogs' conditioned response, a race toward the door from the house to the garage. From there they funneled to the garage clutter past two more cars to the driveway, leaping through the open door of my Honda CRV to the backseat which was reserved especially for them. As usual, B.B. was the first in, having run as fast as she could ahead of Bea. But Miss Bea wasn't far behind, and even though it wasn't graceful, she made the jump in too. Everything else was packed in the available spots in our bursting car.

The upcoming trip would take us across the country to the New England states over several days. We'd be spending nights on the road in many different cities and towns along the way to get way up to Vermont's Northeast Kingdom. Kel and I were very excited about taking what we began to refer to as our first "dog vacation" with them. We knew they both could travel well since we'd taken Kyotee, Bea, and B.B. with us to Boulder, Colorado in the spring of 2000 shortly after B.B. had come to live with us. Since our pack had shrunk again with Kyotee's passing at the ripe old age of 15 1/2 - not bad for an eighty - pound dog - this dog vacation would be just the four of us. Kel and I began to refer affectionately to Bea and B.B. as "the girls" on this first trip, and that stuck through the rest of our many dog vacations. We planned to start out on September twenty-sixth, a Sunday, since Kel had to film a wedding on Saturday down in Duncan, Oklahoma. At this phase of his career he was running a very successful video business, filming many weddings and other events. Of course, we took the girls with us to spend the night in Duncan. We'd bought a new portable dog pen and a tarp to take along on the trip just in case we'd need to corral them at some point, and we'd decided to pack a lot of picnic foods to eat at rest areas along the way so we could all enjoy sitting together at lunch time knowing we wouldn't want to leave the girls in the car while we ate in restaurants. We had assembled a clean-up kit in case of an accident and packed a slew of doggie doo bags. The trip preparations were intense but thrilling in anticipation of the fun we knew we would have. Being in the car and in motel rooms would give us a lot more togetherness with our sweet girls.

That Sunday the plan was to drive home from Duncan and then load up the car with

17

everything for our long-distance trip and drive as far as St. Louis to spend the night in a pet-friendly chain we'd already booked. We had booked dog-friendly places all along the way before we ever set out.

My mother's bright blue weather of October had arrived early, giving us a stunningly sunny, perfect day to travel. Leaving fairly early from Duncan, we got home in plenty of time to pack up again and head for a first night's destination - about a six-hour trip. A blue backpack with a cutting board, knives, plastic forks, spoons, and napkins made up our lunch utilities. I'd emptied an old fruit basket so we could put chips, fruit, nuts, and crackers in it for our lunches. Two small Styrofoam ice chests held all of our cold foods and drinks. All of B.B.'s and Bea's things were packed in several tote bags. Dog beds were thrown in the car loose as well. A little cloth drinking bowl designed for portability made it easy for them to have a drink when we stopped for gas or lunch, and two water bottles filled to the brim provided them with plenty of fresh water. Naturally, Kel and I packed quite a few clothes in two large suitcases, not knowing what the weather would be like where we were going. But now after so many trips, we have come to the conclusion that we never really travel light, no matter our destination.

The girls soon figured out that something was unusual when we arrived home from Duncan, unpacked the car, and then quickly began to pack it up again. Their ears stood up even higher, and their heads were cocked with their eyebrows up and eyes fixed searching our faces as they danced around us while we went up and down the stairs and in and out of the house packing the car. I put their choke chains on and assured them that they'd be going with us by saying the familiar words, "Bea and B.B. go too." I'd said those words many times in the past for shorter car trips. Their tails began to wag furiously as their eyes sparkled and their eyebrows and ears went up in anticipation. Looking at all the bags and assorted things that were gathered in the entry hallway I was afraid that all of it wouldn't fit into the car. But finally, we squeezed the whole mess in making it time for the girls to load up. Luckily, my SUV could hold everything and still leave them plenty of room so they could stretch out or stand up. We took off with big smiles on all of our faces for our first cross-continent dog vacation with the overflowing car looking like the Joads in The Grapes of Wrath.

If we could've harnessed all of the excitement and energy in the car that day, I believe we could've driven to St. Louis without having to buy any gas. The girls stood up nearly all the way because they were so excited and couldn't seem to settle down. We discovered that B. B. liked to bark at the cows and horses out in the fields. We thought it was very funny, so whenever we saw cows, we yelled the word, "Cows!" to her and she barked at them, learning that word very quickly. If Bea was lying down briefly to try and rest a bit, B.B.'s barking would roust her, and she'd bark too even though she didn't have the slightest idea what she was barking at. If the cows were on the other side of the car from where B.B. was standing, she'd trample right over the top of poor Bea to get to that opposite window so she could see them better.

Sometimes they would both lie down, but it was only for a very short time since they'd be up and barking again very soon. There were sure a lot of cows in the fields along the way, or perhaps the loud barking ringing in our ears just made it seem so. When they were worn out from barking, B.B. would lay her head on Bea's back and snuggle together even though they had plenty of room in the backseat.

They both liked to stick their heads out of the windows to breathe in all of the new smells. B.B. got this very dreamy look on her face, and we knew she saw all the things in her head that

her nose was telling her were out there. The glazed faraway look in her eyes told us that she was plotting smell maps. Bea would grin most of the time when she was looking out of the window. If we were next to a car of people, she grinned at them and we laughed. Even those in the other car laughed at her toothy smile if they happened to look sideways and see her eyeing them. By nuzzling Kel's neck very gently, Bea would signal that she needed a break. When she did that, we'd find a place to stop before long.

Leaving by noon, we weren't hungry since we'd eaten a big breakfast at the motel where we'd stayed in Duncan, so we only stopped for gas. The most efficient procedure was for me to pump the gas while Kel got the girls out for a break. Then when he went into the restroom, I gave them a drink from their water bowl. They both lapped up the water at the same time out of the cloth travel bowl, and it was quite funny to watch since the bowl wasn't very big. Then I went to the restroom right before we took off again. We made it in record time to St. Louis before our good Sunday TV shows came on after what turned out to be not a bad drive at all.

I checked us in because we used my credit card on all our trips. Kel got the girls out on their leashes and gave them a break so they'd be ready to eat their supper when they got to the room. Once they were settled in the large room at the La Quinta, we began unloading the car, which went very smoothly. I was so thrilled to be there on this first long dog vacation that I actually jogged down the hallway with a load of bags, even with my bad right hip.

I had suffered with a hip that needed replacement for about twelve years, but I was feeling no pain that evening due to the excitement of our first night on the road on our first dog vacation. Once we got everything into our room, I fed the girls their dry food with just a bit of wet cat food on top to coax them to eat. I always called this their "doggie appetizer." This was mostly for B.B.'s sake, since Bea nearly always ate whatever and whenever she could. She almost never needed to be enticed to eat and barked at B.B. before beginning to eat to keep her away from her food as if B.B. would ever try to eat Bea's food. B.B. was the one who would balk when it came time to eat. She had a rather dicey stomach and often ate grass to purge herself. The doggie appetizer worked most of the time for her, and I had to let Bea have some of it as well. For our supper, easily persuading Kel to just order a pizza to be delivered instead of going out to eat at a restaurant, we were able to stay with the girls and watch the TV shows we always enjoyed on Sunday nights. The girls were given bits of the crusts just like at home. Then after watching some TV, we gave them a short walk close to the motel as their last break before bed, and we all turned in for our first night on the road.

Tucking the girls into their dog beds, I whispered the little poem I always said to them after I kissed them on their smooth heads, "Night-night sleep tight, don't let the bedbugs bite, and I'll see you in the morning bright." It was the same poem my sweet mother had always whispered to me as she tucked me in when I was little. I always kissed B.B. first, then Bea.

We were all so exhausted from the excitement of the day, the loading and unloading and even the driving, so it wasn't long before all four of us were asleep and dreaming of the good things to come. I wondered if B.B. was dreaming of all the cows she'd barked at along the way. Knowing how Bea always loved to eat, she probably dreamed about the delicious pizza crust we'd shared with her.

Chapter 2   Exploring the Morning Glory

This was our longest day of travel. We drove all the way to Pittsburgh, Pennsylvania, which may be why this was not as smooth a drive as on our first day. A couple of small catastrophes didn't stop us from being happy travelers, and the long drive certainly proved to be worth it when we finally arrived at our destination for the night.

There was the usual barking at cows and horses by B.B. with Bea joining in. The scenery was pretty since the leaves had started donning their fall colors. But as we got close to Columbus, Ohio, we got into a huge traffic jam that cost us about thirty minutes. We noticed people in the car next to us laughing and pointing at Bea, and we laughed, too while exchanging looks with them that said, "Yes, we think she's funny too, but we love her dearly." B.B. continued looking for cows, but there were none around, of course, just a sea of cars and trucks.

We stopped for lunch at a rest area near the highway once we cleared the traffic snarl. We were all so glad to be able to stretch our legs and relax a little out of the confinement of the car. Kel tied the girls' leashes to the concrete legs of the picnic table and extended them to their full length so they could walk around. They were both the kind that would extend out about twelve feet and then retract with a brake on them so you could control the length. With those tied to the table leg, the girls were fairly free to sniff around the perimeter. Bea immediately began to let her nose lead her to find anything to eat left there by picnickers in the past. Finding some scrap of food within reach as soon as she started her search, she hurriedly began to gobble it down. Kel scolded her and reached to get the food out of her mouth, fearing that it might be a stray chicken bone or something that might hurt her. But Bea just chomped it to bits as quickly as she could and swallowed the pieces in split seconds, so he couldn't retrieve it. We hoped it wouldn't cause her any trouble later.

B.B. was more interested in smelling where other dogs had been. Roving about like Maypole dancers, they eventually got their long leashes so tangled that neither of them could move. Their faces took on the most forlorn, puzzled expressions mixed with that worried look in their eyes as they strained and tugged on the knotted leashes. It was as if they were saying, "What's happened to us? We were having such a fine time sniffing everything and now we can't move at all. Why aren't you helping us?" They were stuck tight, and it took both of us to untangle them.

Once they were set free, they inevitably wrapped their long leashes around their water bowl, dumping it over. Since they'd already had their fill to drink, it didn't much matter. As we laughed at their antics, Kel fixed sandwiches for our first lunch on the road. Wrapping up our short stop, we headed on to Pittsburgh.

After about four more hours of driving we noticed that B.B. was heaving like she might throw-up. This was not that unusual given her gimpy stomach, or it might've been car sickness due to the length of this drive. I looked for a safe place to pull off of the interstate to try to get her out of the car quickly. I couldn't find a place in time and she threw up a small amount of yellow bile on the backseat. Miss Bea was aghast that B.B. had gotten sick so near to her! Fearing for her beautiful beige coat, she crouched over in the far corner of the backseat against the window where I was afraid she'd fall out if the door hadn't been locked. I finally did find an exit and pulled off. As planned, we had the clean-up kit where we could reach it amidst that sea of stuff, so I cleaned up the bile with a sponge using some of the water we had in the girls' bottles. There really wasn't that much to clean up, thankfully. I gave B.B. a drink of water and we were on our way again. She seemed to feel better after clearing her stomach. We were relieved as well.

24

Leaving these two small catastrophes behind us, we finally pulled into the Morning Glory Inn rather late. We lost an hour since we were now on Eastern Time. The owner left a packet with the key on the front door where we could easily find it. It was a ten-hour-plus drive, so we were all tired, but when we beheld the glorious inn it energized us.

The outside of the large, Gothic building was red brick with clinging ivy draped beautifully up and down on the front. A Mansard roof with lots of windows topped the three-story house, which had a basement as well. When we opened the door and took the girls inside, we discovered, by the absolute stillness that greeted us, that we had the entire place to ourselves! We found our suite upstairs from the front foyer per the landlord's directions that were included in the packet with the key.

"This is gorgeous!" I exclaimed as I looked around. "I can hardly believe our luck!"

"Yeah, I can't even believe the landlord would allow dogs to stay here," Kel marveled. "Are you sure it's ok to have them here?"

"Yes, I checked it online fully before I booked it," I said, easing his concern.

We had a living room, dining area, and bath and then our bedroom was up a lengthy and steep flight of stairs. The furnishings were mostly lovely Victorian antiques with beautiful decor and carpeting. Unloading our car took a full thirty minutes. After the girls were fed their very late supper, B.B. ran right up the stairs to our bedroom with no problem - she even made a game of running up and down them. Since she felt like running about, we knew for sure that she was feeling fine after her little attack of illness earlier in the day. Bea was more reticent as she

25

looked up the long, steep staircase. Noticing that she didn't want to try them, Kel carried her up so she could be with us in the bedroom and explore it. Bea, being older, was not quite as spry as B.B., plus she was heavier due to loving to eat so much and exercising less.

"Let's go on a self-guided tour and creep around to get a look at the entire house since we have the place all to ourselves," I suggested.

We took the girls and prowled around all over the living room downstairs where there was a grand piano. Touring the big kitchen and all through the incredible place was such spooky fun.

But after just a short time I said, " Since it's a Monday night we'd better find a restaurant to eat supper in because the places might close early and it's nearly ten o'clock."

"Yeah, I hope there's something close by since we had such a long drive to get here," Kel agreed.

Fortunately, we found a place not far away where we could eat a delicious Italian dinner. Not surprisingly, they were still open since in Italy, the natives eat late more often than not. We left the girls in the downstairs part of our suite while we were away, knowing that they would be perfect little ladies and not tear up anything or make any messes.

Before we went out the door, I said what I always said upon leaving them, "You girls stay here and take care of this house and we'll be back soon." They knew these words and went from tentative stances to more relaxed prone positions.

As I was turning to leave, I praised them, with a phrase they'd heard many times before, saying, "You're the best of the best, the best in the west and all the rest! The Bestest Dogs in the Whole, Wide World!" It was always true to me.

Getting back around eleven, we found them sleeping peacefully in our living room on the carpet, where they looked like two little angels. Kel carried Bea up to our bedroom again after B.B. had run up there, even passing me when I began climbing the stairs. Their beds had already been placed up there for them to be tucked into, but they shunned them and insisted on curling up on the colorful throw rugs that were scattered around on the carpeted floor which made us laugh. Everyone was very tired but quite contented. Our bed was one of those memory foam mattress types of Swedish beds, very comfortable because it conforms to your body, and we all slept well that night.

Chapter 3   Bea's Selective Hearing

The next morning our landlord arrived early while we were getting dressed, since we'd had such a late night after a long drive. By the time we had walked and fed the girls, he'd fixed us a wonderful breakfast. A very nice man, he was younger than us.

 I asked him, "Would it be okay if I play your grand piano in the living room a little bit?"

He enthusiastically replied," Please do."

So, I played a few Scott Joplin rags that I'd been practicing for fun at home. The piano was in very good condition and quite enjoyable to play. It had already paid off to have my ragtime book along, just in case there might be a piano. Bea and B.B. were listening while cocking their heads sideways with their stand-up ears raised higher than normal. Our landlord and Kel quit visiting and were quietly listening. Kel always loves to hear me play, forgiving the numerous mistakes I make now that I'm out of practice, not playing at school every day.

"We must come back someday and stay for a longer time with the girls," I said.

We had enjoyed our stay at the Morning Glory Inn and hated that it was only for one night.

"Yes, I'd love to do that! I'm sure there are lots of cool things to see and do here," Kel agreed.

But even as I was speaking, a quote from the poem, "The Road Not Taken," by Robert Frost came drifting into my mind. Set to music, our Concert Choir had performed a version when I was a senior in high school and sang in the soprano section. The words of a particular phrase fit our current situation perfectly and meant more to me now than back when I'd sung it in the choir: "Yet knowing how way leads on to way, I doubted if I should ever come back."

The farther northeast we went, the more brightly colored trees we encountered. The weather was cooler, too, so we could have the windows open for the girls to breathe in all of the smells. Once we got out of the city there was plenty of farmland which meant there were also plenty of horses and cows for B.B. to bark at along the way. We noticed that she, perhaps, never really made the distinction between them. If it had four legs and was large, she would begin barking. So, if we spotted horses grazing in a field, we began to distinguish them by saying, "Horsiecows!" to let her know there was something to bark at, but it wasn't a just a cow. As long as we followed the word of the animal's actual name with the word "cows" she recognized that word and barked. She even barked at "goatcows" and "sheepcows" as we drove on. B.B. let them all know she was in the area by barking with no discrimination. But having become used

28

to traveling, both girls were quicker now about settling down in the car and resting a little more in between the barking episodes.

It was a fairly long drive, and we arrived at our motel long after the sun had set that night. We had to unload the car and get the girls all settled into the room in the darkness. Our room there was no Morning Glory Inn. It was a small room in Albany at a Motel 6, but it was clean, and the quality was good enough. After feeding the girls. Kel and I went out to eat at a restaurant.

Every time Kel and I went out to go eat or sightsee or whatever we might do without the girls, we'd leave the TV on, so they'd not hear the noises outside the room so clearly. This would keep them from barking and disturbing anyone else who was staying there. Bea had more selective hearing the older she got. She'd hear if she wanted to and ignore what she didn't want to hear. When Kel scolded her for eating food off the ground, she chose to ignore him. We could tell that she was hearing him - her behavior gave her away when she hurried to swallow before he could fish it out of her mouth. She could nearly always hear the sound of people walking by and talking outside of the motel room if we didn't have the TV on, and she'd bark, so it was better to leave it on. B.B. had great hearing still and, taking her watchdog job very seriously, would always bark if she was alarmed by someone outside the door. But with the TV on, she didn't notice sounds outside of the room either. We never once had anyone complain about our girls barking. Regardless of their hearing capabilities, the girls' ears smelled fresh and clean. They were able to express many different feelings by the actions they could make those ears do. I would stick my nose in them and sniff deeply. "I wish I could bottle that smell and keep it in a jar!" I declared one day.

Chapter 4   Bob Newhart's Inn

Excitement fueled us knowing we'd be taking the scenic route to drive on the Mohawk Trail while making our way to Vermont. This is the historic path that so many famous people traveled on through Massachusetts. Taking an interest in history - Kel had earned a master's degree in history - we wanted to see it for ourselves. Also, we were looking forward to visiting our new friends, Tim and Kathleen, whom we'd met on our trip to Ireland in August when they'd been on the same walking tour.

In Ireland I told them, "We're planning to drive to Vermont in late September to see the beautiful autumn leaves."

Kathleen had promptly responded, "Then we'd love to have you come to our home for dinner during your stay."

Accepting their generous invitation right away, Kel let them in on a secret, saying, "If you invite Okies to visit you, they will definitely show up!"

One more thing made this day, September 29, special - it was our son, Jeff's birthday. He's actually my stepson, but he has always called me Mom ever since he and his dad came to live with me. In fact, Jeff was my student in music class before I ever met his dad, and he was the one who introduced us.

30

Kel had been unable to find a babysitter, so he just brought Jeff to the all-adult birthday party with him. When I saw Jeff walk in, I recognized him at once, and he wasted no time in introducing me to his dad. Later, Kel asked me out and we've been together ever since. It was my pleasure to have played a role in raising Jeff since, if given a choice, I thought he was the one I would've picked to be my son!

We were sorry that we weren't there to celebrate with him. But I assured him, "We can celebrate with you once we arrive back home."

He replied, "I'll probably celebrate it with my friends or my sister in Tulsa, so don't worry about it."

"You're a good son," I complimented, which always made him smile.

The scenery was eye-popping everywhere we looked with the leaves in full turn providing views like giant landscape paintings as we sped along. The sun made the leaves sparkle and their colors shine more brilliantly. The air was cool, so we rolled the windows down again for the girls to sniff. Resembling a scene out of a Norman Rockwell painting, Kel captured lots of old buildings and churches in the small towns with the brightly colored leaves framing them in the many photos he took. There were also photos of each other with our girls against the backdrop of tidy houses and hillsides ablaze with color.

Kel mused, "I'm so impressed with how clean everything is. There's not a speck of trash on the ground or the roadside."

"Yeah, I wish it was that way in Oklahoma," I added. Our state has a big litter problem, even though the anti-litter motto encourages people to "Keep Our Land Grand" by disposing of trash correctly. But there's always hope for the future.

Brattleboro proved to be a pretty little town to explore that afternoon. The girls enjoyed walking around with us for a while and sniffing everything in their path as they looked at all of the other tourists who were shopping. After a little while we thought we could probably leave them in the car for a short time as long as the windows were slightly open since the weather was so pleasant and cool. "Miss Bea might be getting tired from all the walking," I said, since I'd observed her pace slowing considerably.

So, we locked them in the backseat leaving the windows cracked for a half hour while we shopped some more. If anyone came near, B.B. would bark and then Bea would join in. We theorized that no one would bother any of our stuff since B.B. always looked fierce and vicious when she barked, even though she really wasn't. Our shopping ended and it was on to Middlebury, so we'd be on time for the dinner party.

Tim and their son, Collin, were waiting for us at the Waybury Inn when we arrived to check in as the sun was just beginning to disappear beyond the horizon. The Waybury is where they filmed the Bob Newhart TV show using the outside with the big front porch as a backdrop for any outdoor shots of Bob's fictional inn.

The main porch had rocking chairs lined up in a row, sheltered by the ceiling of the second floor, just begging you to sit a spell and enjoy relaxing there. Around the corner at another entrance there is a bright green awning with Waybury Inn printed on it. The structure is set

32

perfectly among some lovely big trees that were changing into their fall colors.

After he gave them a good break under those trees, Kel and the girls took advantage of that big front porch while I checked us in. Seeing them there when I came out with our keys to the room, I took a photo of Kel sitting in one of the rocking chairs with the leashed girls standing at his feet, and all three grinning from ear to ear.

The place was decorated for autumn and Halloween inside and out and was neat as a pin. It was even better than what we'd expected. Our room was all the way to the top of the third floor, up the main staircase and to the left. Fortunately, Bea had no trouble with the wide stairs inside. Naturally, B.B. ran up them very quickly. They were on leashes so they couldn't just take off on their own to sniff everything around them, possibly breaking some of the beautiful antiques that fill the place. Their lobby is very cozy and inviting, decorated so beautifully with warm wood paneling, two huge fireplaces made of native stone on either end, lights that give off a soft golden glow and the exquisite antiques.

"I can hardly believe our luck that they allow dogs to stay in such a nice place!" I exclaimed. As we passed through, we noticed a photo that was signed by Bob Newhart: "To Tracey, Take care of my inn! Bob Newhart." In it he sports his famous smile and has his arms crossed – the way we'd seen him so many times on his show.

That impressed us since we are fans, always enjoying the characters and the clever deadpan delivery and humor. Our room was just as nice as the rest of the place. Conveniently, there is a back staircase on the outside of the building that we used to take the girls in and out rather than traipsing back and forth like a parade through the lobby every time. It is up so high that I feared we might have trouble getting Bea up and down the steep stairs, but after holding back at first, she learned fairly quickly how to negotiate them and showed no fear, just caution. My fear of heights made me as careful as Bea when descending those stairs, and I had to slow B.B. down to a walk so she wouldn't drag us both down. We followed Tim and his handsome teen-aged son to their home, which wasn't very far. Kathleen was waiting with take-out from a Thai restaurant. It was wonderful to see them again and get to know Collin. Being in their lovely home was enjoyable, and we had fun visiting with all three of them. Some of our time was spent reminiscing about Ireland and our tour over there. The food was delicious - we're big Thai lovers because of the spicy, hot flavors and their expertise with tofu. They enhanced the meal with wine. Kel laughingly reminded them that, "If you invite Okies to visit you, they will definitely show up." That had certainly proven to be true, and we all laughed. The time flew by like the autumn leaves in the wind, and we said a fond farewell to go back to the girls.

"If you ever come to Oklahoma, we'd love for you to stop in and have dinner with us." I extended the invitation before parting.

Since Kel was our navigator, we had no trouble finding our way back. Being a Boy Scout when he was growing up, he learned to landmark, so he was easily able to direct me. I'm not sure that I would've been able to find my way back without him as I'm not at all good with directions and forget to landmark most of the time.

34

Upon our arrival back, and after checking on the girls, we tiptoed down the grand staircase to the cozy bar where we each ordered an Irish Coffee as a nightcap. A drink we learned how to make while on our trip to Ireland, we had developed a taste for it.

Kel, my night owl, proposed, "Since it's such a quiet, crisp night, would you want to take the girls out on a longer walk in the moonlight?"

"Sounds good to me. I need to burn some calories after all that I've consumed today."

Bundled up in our jackets, we spent forty-five minutes walking around the area with the girls who were more than happy to sniff the plentiful foliage all along the way while the moon and stars shone brightly down on us in the clear dark sky. Fall was certainly evident in the cool, clean air. It was quite late when we finally herded the girls back up the steep outside staircase and into our room where we all settled down for a restful sleep. What a magical evening it had been.

Chapter 5   The Girls Get a Canoe Ride

Loading the car became a routine, and like in the military, we all four knew the drill. It was similar to putting a puzzle together in that everything fit in a particular place at a particular time. I was the sergeant with Kel as my soldier. My job was to make sure every piece of our stuff was put in exactly the right spot in the car in the correct sequence. To do otherwise might risk being unable to fit it all in or having to remove something to put the correct piece in place. Following this procedure made the packing go quickly.

The girls knew the routine by now and weren't afraid of being left behind. As we went in and out of our rooms putting the car puzzle together, they sat watching and waiting patiently for us to say the magic words, "Car-Car," before they'd jump up to go. It became a race between the two of them to see who could jump in first. We felt like we were dog skiing since it was difficult to hold them back on their leashes. Being strong, fifty-pound dogs, they pulled hard on whichever one of us took them out. Before we let them really have their head, like a team of tiny horses, we made sure we cleared the building and were on level ground.

"Little Horse" was one of Bea's many nicknames long before we came on this trip, because in a strange way she resembled a small, orange Shetland pony. However, B.B. always won the race and leaped into the car just barely ahead of Bea, since she was younger, thinner, and faster. Bea was older, slower and heavier due to her love of eating, but never gave up trying, so there were times when it was almost a tie.

That last day of September, the weather was perfectly glorious for viewing the foliage as we motored through the villages of Willoughvale and Orleans to Lake Willoughby. We got a fairly early start from the Waybury Inn; we were sorry that we hadn't booked a longer stay at that lovely place. The deeper we went into Vermont, the more the leaves made hillsides into rainbow mosaics.

"I can't believe how beautiful this scenery is!" I exclaimed.

"Yeah, I hope these photos on the fly will show it for how lovely it really is," Kel agreed.

We called it "on the fly" because he snapped photos while the car sped down the highway, because I didn't want to stop very often. My desire to get to Lake Willoughby at a reasonable time was the force driving my foot on the gas pedal. After all, we were only going to be there for one night, so we had to get there as quickly as possible to make the most of our short time. We flew past quaint country lanes wondering where they went. After a while we stopped by a lovely field to give the girls a chance to sniff and relieve themselves. They were very happy about that, as big smiles lit up their faces due to so many new smells. But there was little time to spend exploring around.

In the middle of the afternoon we pulled into the Willoughvale Inn, built on the shores of Lake Willoughby. After I checked us in, we took the girls way up two flights of stairs to our room named the Weathervane at the very highest point of the place.

It was a lovely big room with a view of glistening Lake Willoughby out of one of our several large windows. The rolling hills across the lake were exquisite, showing off their many colors of leaves. The room was beautifully decorated in neutral colors with pleasant pictures hung on the walls, and delicate curtains at each window in the same neutral colors had a splash of yellow, green, and blue flowers on them. It was a bright and cheery room furnished with a large queen bed near the door, a sitting area across by two of the big windows with two soft comfortable chairs, and a writing desk with a straight-backed chair against a wall, where you could sit and see out of yet another large window. A TV and a big bathroom completed it.

Out a side window of our room was a large weathervane perched at the highest point on the roof of a turret level with our line of sight. At the top of the weathervane, which was in the shape of a cross, was an arrow pointing skyward. On the left horizontal part was a cow flying

37

high in the air and staring towards another arrow pointing outwards opposite of her.

"I wonder why they'd put a cow on a weathervane," Kel mused. "It seems like such an odd thing to put so high up in the air."

"Maybe it was the cow who jumped over the moon in 'Hey Diddle Diddle,' " I responded as an old elementary music teacher would.

While the girls slept in the room, we discovered some dusty old bicycles parked near the back door. The innkeeper informed us that they were for guests, and we were welcome to ride them if we desired. On the last full day of our group tour in Ireland our leader, Noel, had put everyone on bikes to ride around on Valentia Island. When we discovered we could still ride bicycles we were hooked. It wasn't long after we came back from overseas, we purchased hybrids in Tulsa. Riding those on short rides of two miles or so, we'd been getting used to bicycling, but had left them at home as there was no way to transport them on the car.

Quickly deciding it would be fun to ride the inn's old bicycles to see a little more of the countryside, we inspected them. They didn't look like they'd been ridden in quite a while and didn't have as many gears as our new bicycles at home. But they had brakes and the tires were filled, so we set off down the road to see where it would lead. For safety we always wore helmets but hadn't brought them on the trip. Luckily the innkeeper kindly loaned us two.

Shortly, we came upon the small village of Willoughvale. Stopping for some pictures in front of their little white church set among the shelter of the colorful trees, I posed in a serene little park next to a bench across from the church. The photo reflects the clean air, the bright blue sky, and my enjoyment of our ride. Later, I snapped a shot of Kel while he stood with the bicycle by a house which was painted crimson with white curtains at the windows. Behind it was a smaller white house with the gleaming hills rising up majestically in the background. Since Kel and I hadn't been riding very far at home and were not the seasoned bicycle riders that we are now, even a small knoll was a challenge for me.

There came a point in our short trek when I was struggling to climb a hill. The hill was winning this one, and I was seething with frustration watching Kel disappear ahead of me in the distance. He'd been able to get up and over the hill without much difficulty. Part of my trouble was that I'd chosen to put off the hip operation because I never wanted to stop being active for the six to eight weeks it would take to recover. This hill had pushed me to my limit.

With my anger growing as I struggled to pedal, I yelled out, "I can't make it up this damn hill! What are you trying to do, kill me? This is too hard! I want to go back!"

 Kel, hearing me cry out, burst back up over the top of the hill, then coasted down to try and smooth things over. My mind was made up, and I wouldn't hear of going farther, so regretfully, we retraced our path on the lonely highway. Shedding the bicycle along with my bad mood, once we were back and saw our precious girls, I felt relieved. I apologized to Kel for my outburst; he forgave me, and everything was forgotten as we looked around for what we could do next.

Our eyes lit upon bobbing canoes on the glassy surface of the lake luring us to try them out. Like the bikes, these were available to guests, complete with life preservers. As I'm not a strong swimmer, I was more than happy to wear a life preserver. Kel didn't mind wearing one either, even though he'd swum on his high school team many years before.

The girls had never been in a canoe. Bea had a look of trepidation on her face as we made her follow an also-suspicious-B.B. into the waiting canoe from the dock. Just getting them into the rocking vessel was a major accomplishment. Once we got to rowing, though, both girls seemed to be enjoying being out on the water. Bea even had on her big broad shit-eating grin. I sat in the bow with the girls between us in the middle while Kel sat with the camera in the stern so he could steer and take lots of photos of all three of us and the abundant scenery lining the banks. There were neat wooden homes, mostly painted white, adorning the shores which made a lovely contrast against the gleaming red, yellow, orange, green, and deep violet hues of the leaves on the large trees surrounding them. Scattered between the houses would be a red or green building and docks with all kinds of boats floating in the quiet water or beached upon the shore. Under the impression we both were rowing as we got way out in the lake, I turned around to discover that Kel, instead of paddling, was taking photos of me rowing and the girls' expressions. "Foul!" I yelled as I wrinkled my brow at him.

"Well I just thought since you're part Cherokee, you'd be an expert at rowing!" he teased. "I thought you'd be able to do ALL the rowing!"

"Oh, is that so?" I retorted. "You'd better put down that camera and pick up that oar if you know what's good for you!"

We shared a laugh since we both knew that, unfortunately, I wasn't schooled in

40

ANYTHING Native American. My daddy grew up in a time when being even a small percentage of Cherokee was looked down upon. He and my mother had spoken of how he was bullied as a young boy before he learned how to defend himself. After that mistreatment and discrimination, it was no wonder he'd chosen to ignore the Native American culture. The sad experiences he had walking home from school every day made him somewhat ashamed of his heritage.

Kel put the camera down and both of us rowed. We were all having a good time as we traveled down the lake for what seemed like several miles until I glanced over at B.B. who had a dire look on her face with her ears flattened on either side of her head. Lucky I checked her out when I did because no sooner had I turned around to look at her when she began to retch and heave. There was no doubt that she was going to throw up. Not wanting her to vomit into the bottom of the boat, I quickly grabbed her by the collar and held her head over the side. I barely forced her snout out towards the water with her head clear of the inside of the boat when she threw up a little stream of yellow bile, the same as she had in the car on our way to Pittsburgh. Seasickness had hit our poor Little Sprite! Once she cleared her stomach she perked right up, and her face took on that dreamy expression as she enjoyed the rest of the ride. Bea, who was always immaculate with her appearance, was very upset by B.B.'s brief bout of illness. Her toothy smile vanished, and she wrinkled her brow with worry. Eventually, it was forgotten as we sailed along admiring the view of all the pretty houses and trees. Making it back with no more incidents, we were able to get the girls out of the canoe rather awkwardly, but unscathed. It had

41

been a fun ride overall.

Chapter 6   The Bread and Puppet

Before the morning was half over, we were on our way to New Hampshire and the Chesterfield Inn out in the countryside, named for the small hamlet nearby. We didn't have a GPS, so all of our driving directions were printed from the computer at home, plus our trusty atlas was packed in the front seat area just in case. Kel guided me expertly as we drove along the rural roads and past small country lanes. Stopping to inspect a covered bridge, the first one I'd ever seen, I readily imagined Ichabod Crane spurring his horse, Gunpowder, to urge him to move as fast as the poor old nag could go as he tried to beat the Headless Horseman to the bridge. Passing by farmers' fields we saw the rolled bales of hay ready to be stored away in the barns for the cows and horses to eat throughout the long winter. The farms were tidy, and most of the barns were red, just as we expected. Always the multi-colored leaves provided eye candy for us, and the cows and horses grazing in their bucolic fields broke the monotony for the girls.

We hadn't gone very far when we spied a sign advertising the Bread and Puppet Museum. Kel was vaguely familiar with the name of the street theatre group but really didn't know much else about what it was. Not wanting to let the chance to stop in and see the puppets pass us by, we pulled into their dooryard. A sign saying the entry is free, but donations would be accepted hung near the entrance. We left the car in the shade with the windows rolled halfway down so the girls would stay nice and cool on that pleasant morning with mild temperatures and a slight breeze. No one was around to let us in, but the door was unlocked, so in we went.

42

What an incredible place! Two huge barns were filled to the brim with puppets that ran the gamut from gigantic to tiny. Most of the puppet scenes had a political significance to them. Some portrayed real people of the past, and the majority represented the liberal ideals of the 1960s and 1970s. Many were posed acting out scenes of protest or true events with lots of them having explanatory scripts or dialogue on signs nearby. The larger ones were just downright scary, the stuff of nightmares. There were those made of paper mache and painted bright colors, and quite a few with sad, deadpan faces. There were even a bunch with a white ghostlike appearance. Puppets with noses, mouths, and ears but no eyes were quite disturbing. A good many of them were animal puppets.

One scene involved the killing of a horse who was life-size. B.B. would've probably barked at it if she'd been allowed inside to see it. The men doing the killing were life-size as they were all suspended in action. There was a giant green and red dragon with its humongous teeth threatening from its open mouth while its shark's eyes stared. Not a blank nook or cranny was to be found as every available space had been filled with some kind of puppet display. They were packed into the barn as tightly as our stuff was packed into our car. It nearly overloaded my senses.

After about an hour of viewing the scenes and reading some of the explanatory scripts, I felt like I was in Hell yet enjoying every minute of it. But instead of being hot, I shivered, feeling how really cold it was, as if the grisly spirits of some of the people long dead portrayed by the puppets were loitering about.

Sometimes I had the feeling that I was being watched. It was weird and creepy but at the same time astounding and exhilarating, especially since we were the only ones meandering around in there for the first hour. The eerie silence and the crowd of blank staring eyes made a chill trickle right down my back.

"This reminds me of Dante's Inferno and the Rings of Hell," Kel confided to me as we wound our way through the cold atmosphere of the ghostly barn.

The biggest puppets were over twenty feet tall dwarfing us as we looked up at them in wonder. The tiniest were maybe two inches. That the artists and craftsmen were able to construct them in such a minuscule size was amazing to me.

Puppets with devil-like horns that were a metallic bronze color, and more with disturbing green faces and slitty eyes that had no pupils were frightening. Even one giant puppet glared down, looking just like I would imagine Old Ned himself would look looming over us at no less than twenty feet tall.

Kel was in heaven! Besides furiously snapping photos, he used his video camera and filmed everything from top to bottom. Unless he captured nearly all of that horde on film, I knew it would be hard to get him to leave. He's the kind of man who wants to study the products at the grocery store in depth, so I had no doubt that he'd want to see every last puppet no matter how petite. If we'd be able to arrive at a reasonable time to the Chesterfield Inn, I'd have to be the one to call a halt at some point. Trying to be patient, I let him linger to film to his heart's content even when I was ready to leave.

Our tour took well over two hours through the two barn museums marveling at the immensity of it all. It was not nearly long enough, but knowing we had to drive on, we dragged ourselves out of our emergence in the past and left a small donation in their jar by the door. By then other people were looking through the barns.

It left my head full and spinning with the astonishing images. Would I be visited in my dreams tonight by some of those ghoulish characters? It didn't matter, since I wouldn't have missed seeing them for the world. It was one of those rare unplanned opportunities that just popped up along the way that can be even more fun than the stops you've carefully planned out.

The road took us through many small, picturesque towns that are thriving, unlike so many in our own state that seem to be literally dying right before our eyes as the elderly pass away and the younger ones leave to find work in larger cities.

One Vermont village in particular was so quaint and compelling that we decided to stop there to spend a little time and look around a bit. As the girls and I sat on a bench near their white church, looking like it had been plucked right out of a Norman Rockwell painting, the bells chimed the noon hour. This town called Peacham is the "Most Photographed Small Town in Vermont," according to a sign we saw. It was easy to see why. Everywhere we turned, a scene of idyllic beauty met our eyes, whether it was a home, a red barn, or a white church with a high pointed steeple and bell tower. They all had been embraced by the painter's palette of brightly colored leaves on the stately trees near them. And nearly every house exhibited an autumn display somewhere close to it with scarecrows, pumpkins, gourds, wheat, or bales of hay much

45

like mine back home.

After the bells chimed twelve o'clock, they played hymns for about five minutes, a sort of mini concert during the lunch hour. I enjoyed the sweet strains of the music, but the girls paid no attention whatsoever to the tunes. Instead Bea busied herself with hunting around the bench for food that might've been dropped by someone in the past who'd eaten lunch there. B.B., nose to the ground, was able to pick up the scent of the squirrels, rabbits, and other dogs who'd stopped there. Kel hastily took photos all around the area.

That afternoon we arrived in Montpelier, the capital of Vermont. It certainly wasn't what I expected a capital city to look like. We'd been in other state capitals in large cities. This was a fairly small town by comparison, with a homey atmosphere we liked right away, feeling quite comfortable as we walked around there with the girls. By mid-afternoon we were hungry, so after settling the girls where we knew they would be fine in the car since the weather was so crisp and pleasant, we began the search for a place to eat a bite of lunch.

Being vegetarians makes it a challenge sometimes for us to find a suitable place to eat. We're not really fond of just eating salads all the time. What really makes us boycott a place is when we ask a waitress if they have any vegetarian choices on their menu and she tells us that they can just leave the meat off of a particular dish so that it becomes their idea of a vegetarian meal. Then if the offer isn't made to reduce the price when the meat is left off, we assume they'll still charge us the same price as if the meat were on it. That really makes us angry and leaves us feeling penalized for being vegetarians.

46

I spotted a diner across the street from where we'd parked the car and suggested, "Maybe that diner over there will have a vegan burger or some kind of veggie sandwich that we can eat."

"I don't know - it IS a diner," he said skeptically as he looked where I was pointing.

"But this IS Vermont. We're not in Beef Country Oklahoma anymore," I reminded him.

I persuaded him to at least check out the posted menu. While standing in the doorway scanning their offerings we were delightfully surprised by the abundance of vegetarian and even vegan choices. We quickly decided to go in and eat but deciding what to order took a lot longer due to the plethora of tantalizing vegetarian options. This was a new experience for us in the twelve years we'd been vegetarians. Ironically, we both ordered the same thing - the veggie burgers with fries. Considering that the lunch hour was long over, quite a large crowd was eating there, so we were glad that it didn't take long before we were served our luscious lunch as deliciously flavorful as we expected. This was our kind of diner.

Satisfied, we took the girls out for a little walk around the downtown area before loading them back into the car for the rest of the drive to New Hampshire. As it was beginning to get dark, we arrived at the Chesterfield Inn just a little bit over the border into New Hampshire. When we checked into our lovely cottage that was set apart from the rest of the inn, we had to pinch ourselves to make sure we weren't dreaming.

It was spacious with a four-poster bed so tall that they had to provide a footstool to climb into it! There was a homey fireplace, a small refrigerator, and a porch out front with a wooden

bench for sitting under the shelter of the sloping roof. The decor was all very tasteful, with a

large area rug covering most of the floor. A good-sized bathroom contained a wonderful claw-

foot tub. Beautiful lamps graced bedside tables, and comfortable easy chairs invited lounging.

We were glad there was no television or phone to distract us. Outside on the grass in front of the

place were two wooden, low-slung lawn chairs. Large trees in a variety of colors enclosed the

cottage like clasped hands. Up a slight hill about fifty feet was the two-stories-tall main building

of the inn. A good-sized balcony on the second story faced out towards our cottage. An old, rustic barn on the property behind the inn glowed orange in the setting sun, as did the short thick grasses hugging it. A small pond out farther in front of our cottage with cattails, reeds and tall grasses surrounding its shores made the whole yard look like something out of a tourist brochure. We couldn't believe our good fortune finding such a beautiful place to stay that allowed our dogs to stay with us. We were so happy that we'd booked it for two nights so we could enjoy all it had to offer. We unloaded the girls, and they busied themselves with sniffing all around, Bea looking for leftover food and B.B. looking for small animals to chase. The two of us decided to drive across the border back into Vermont to eat dinner in the small village of Putney.

I'd read about it in a book we'd purchased before the trip that told about many places to visit and things to see. It was one of those places that the author was encouraging "leaf peepers" not to miss. So, we ate spinach salads for supper at a diner over there. It was a pleasant surprise that even this small village diner had a lot of vegetarian items on their menu. We'd thought it was just a fluke when we'd eaten such wonderful vegetarian fare at the diner in the capital city.

There really wasn't much else to see in tiny Putney, and we questioned why the author had recommended it so highly. Taking a quick look around the little burg, which didn't take long since it had just one main street, we were satisfied that we hadn't missed anything important, and made the short drive back over to our superior cottage across the border in New Hampshire. Kel lit a warm fire in the fireplace, and we basked in front of it, relaxing with our girls and reminiscing about what we'd seen and done that day. The warmth of the fire hastened our drowsiness making us ready for bed. What a wonderfully cozy place. How could it be any better than this? After getting into the soft bed, we mused about how the first half of this trip had gone swimmingly for the most part, with just a few little bumps in the road. The worst things that had happened were B.B.'s bouts of car and sea sickness. But the more she traveled the better she felt. Thankfully, she hadn't gotten ill anymore.

This was the midway point on our first dog vacation. After our stay here, we'd be turning to start wending our way home. On this night with the fire blazing a golden red glow, and the flickering flames looking like some of the puppets' faces we'd seen earlier in the day, I wondered aloud, "This is the best trip, better than any ever! How could tomorrow outdo today?" As the fire burned lower and we drifted off into a contented slumber, little did we know that we were about to find out.

Chapter 7   The Kancamagus and The Catastrophe

The Kancamagus Highway is one of the most scenic byroads to view fall foliage, so we definitely wanted to drive it, but we would not be able to leave the girls inside the cottage for as long as we'd be gone. It takes a while to get to that particular section of road since Kel would want to stop along the way for photos. I didn't want him to take pictures on the fly when this promised to be some of the best scenery. So, our only option was to take the girls along on this adventure - something we were happy to do. We encountered a heavier drizzle the farther north we drove, but Kel and I didn't mind since it fit the spooky mood of the White Mountain National

Forest we passed through, and made the car feel much snugger and cozier. Even though it was a cloudy gray day, the views were spectacular. Stopping at the Swift River to give the girls a short break, there was a flurry of picture-taking. Since it was a Saturday, quite a lot of other tourists were traveling the same way.

The "Kanc," as it's commonly referred to by the locals, took us to an elevation of nearly 3000 feet when we reached the summit at Kancamagus Pass, on the side of Mount Kancamagus near Lincoln. The drizzle now turned to a harder rain, but we were undaunted in our quest to see as much as possible. The other peepers were out in full force as well to fill their souls with the beauty of nature's magic wand that had waved over the leaves. Granted, we missed out on the leaves sparkling brilliantly if the sun had been shining, but there was something extremely mystical about the deep smells of the heavy forests in the somber atmosphere of that drab day. The sweet-smelling rain gave us a uniquely dreamy portrait of the Kancamagus Scenic Byway.

The girls had a wonderful time with the windows rolled down enough for them to stick their noses out and breathe in the many scents of the forests. I easily imagined how the Native Americans lived here, hunting, fishing, and teaching their children all of their ways and culture. Then the hardy pioneers worked the land here, living on small farms in cabins they built on the hillsides tucked into the notches.

It is pleasantly surprising to see no filling stations, restaurants, hotels, or other businesses marring that short stretch. The mind wanders constructing scenes from the way it used to be centuries ago.

"Since we've taken our time along the way, I think we should start back once we get to the end of the Kanc," I suggested. Reluctantly, but wisely, he agreed with me. Of course, once we got done with the 34 1/2 miles of pure scenery, the places to eat, stay, and get gas began to appear.

On the return we stopped at Crawford Notch to check out where a tragedy had happened. In 1825 a man by the name of Samuel Willey, Jr. built a small cabin at the foot of what's now called Mount Willey. He had a wife and five children. Everything went well for a while until a prolonged drought killed off the vegetation in 1826 followed by a very substantial rain. The Saco River, which has its headwaters in Crawford Notch, came twenty feet out of its banks during the night. With no foliage, the shifting conditions caused a horrific landslide.

Two days after the terrible flood friends made an awful discovery. The Willey cabin was intact untouched by the huge landslide. A large ridge had divided the landslide, so its course flowed around the rustic house carrying debris and large boulders with it. Their horrified friends found the dead bodies of Mr. and Mrs. Willey along with two of their children among the boulders. The three other children were missing, never to be found.

Nathaniel Hawthorne wrote a famous story about that particular notch and the family who perished there. Kel had read the story, so we had to see where this sad event occurred. Then we read more at the site about the Willey cottage which, after their deaths, had stood as an inn for travelers until 1898 when it caught fire and was destroyed. The site was now marked by a large boulder and a bronze plaque. The chilly, grave day with misting rain seemed appropriate for our visit, enhancing the scariness of the catastrophe that had happened so long ago.

Since it was still raining Kel made a little joke, "Wow, I hope there hasn't been a drought here lately!"

The girls enjoyed sniffing all around the area as they were being cooed over and petted by the many other tourists. One woman asked me, "What breed of dogs are they?" This wasn't the first time that question had been asked. Since they looked so much alike except for their color, many people assumed they were a specific newer breed.

I answered her with what Kel and I had decided upon, saying in all seriousness, "They're Shep Peis." She gave me a rather quizzical look but seemed satisfied with my answer. Once we all were loaded in the car, we had a moment of levity regarding that encounter after all the solemnity we'd just been through.

Twilight came upon us sooner than we realized since night's curtain is lowered earlier at this time of year. Kel was navigating to find the quickest route back due to the growing darkness and my anxiousness to be at the cottage. The girls were tired and cuddled up in the middle of the backseat together to nap a bit. It was the same position as always when traveling - Bea's head resting near the front edge of the backseat with her body stretched out in a vertical sort of way with her butt touching the back of the seat, while B.B.'s head cradled itself on the upper part of Bea's back with her body horizontally across the back of the seat to Bea's left resembling two angels. Seeing them sleeping so peacefully inspired Kel and me to make plans for how we would spend the evening once we made it to the cozy warmth of our beautiful cottage.

"Let's get a bite to eat over in Putney once we get back and I take care of the girls. I'll feed them then give them a short walk," I said.

"Sounds good. I'll make a fire in the fireplace so we can cuddle with the girls in front of it when we get back from eating supper," he added.

"I think we should open that bottle of red wine we've been saving. It seems like the perfect occasion to sip it, don't you think?" I asked hopefully.

My tender husband agreed that the wine would complement the evening while we watched the ever-changing visions in the flames and discussed all the marvelous scenery and events of the day - a truly romantic evening for all four of us.

Once we settled on our plans, the drive seemed to take forever in the pitch blackness of the starless night. I tried to be extremely cautious so as not to hit a deer that might suddenly dash in front of the car as there were warning signs all along the way about deer and moose. It was a stressful journey, but, thankfully, we never saw any.

It was a race to drop the girls at our cabin with their food and water and then speed over to Putney for a quick pizza - same place as before since there weren't many to choose from - and back around 9:30. It was time to slow the evening down with some love and leisure - the thought thrilled me.

After leashing the girls, we took off out of the cottage door. I noticed there were six or more people crowded onto a small balcony on the second floor of the main inn as the night had turned out to be rather nice once the rain ended. They looked like they were having a merry old time: eating, drinking, laughing, and visiting

When I walked both girls by myself, I always held B.B.'s leash in my left hand, and she was on point trotting along faster ahead of Bea and me. Bea's leash was always in my right hand, since she moved more slowly and was usually about two feet behind me. I guided them through the lighted areas, so we were able to see where we were walking. We'd only gone a short distance before I turned my head to see Miss Bea assume that hunched over position. Just then, I felt such an unexpected strong tug on B.B.'s leash that I lost my grip as she jerked it right out of my hand. This alarmed me. Normally, if the leash got dropped accidentally it would scare her, and she'd stop immediately and give me a quizzical look until I picked it up again to resume walking. But there was no stopping her this time. As quick as thought, I turned by head to look in B.B.'s direction just in time to witness her running away at break-neck speed.

"B.B., stop!" I yelled with as much authority as I could muster.

The lights shining on the field in front of our cottage were just bright enough for me to discern that her mouth was wide open ready to attack. She was at a dead run when it appeared that she was hit full in the face - eyes, ears, nose, gaping mouth, chin, neck, and chest - with the putrid spray of none other than a fluffy black and white-striped skunk! Just as quickly as she'd dashed over to it, she whirled like a little black tornado and began a hasty retreat back to me coughing and sputtering while dragging her long, extended leash behind her. Meanwhile, the skunk made his own retreat for the safety of the bushes by the pond. My only hope was that maybe the skunk had been a bad shot and missed her. But as she rapidly drew nearer to where Bea and I were standing in stunned silence, the pristine Miss Bea, who had already picked up the pungent odor, confirmed to me by her avoidance of B.B., that, indeed the skunk had perfect aim. A few seconds later, the unmistakable scent hit me like a punch in the nose.

Now Bea was the dog who kept her fur so nice and clean. She never rolled in manure like Rapport had always done when we went to a farm area where cattle or horses had grazed, or never stepped in any mud like B.B. quite often did on rainy walks. She didn't even really like to swim like Jade and Kyotee had because it mussed up her beautiful orange fur coat. So, it was no surprise that she kept her distance and would have nothing to do with the now reeking B.B.

I felt so sorry for my sweet little B.B. as I saw from her pawing at them that her eyes must be burning and stinging. The stench filling her keen nose was unbearable as she snorted and sneezed, and the taste in her mouth sickened her since she was gagging between the snorts! She rubbed her chin and face on my legs while she coughed and sputtered. Now I, too smelled like

56

skunk!

My brain froze - I literally couldn't think! It was a blank inside my mind until I began to speak these five words, "What-am-I-gonna-do? What-am-I-gonna-do? What-am-I-gonna-do?" If I said them once, I said them a hundred times, and they became my mantra as the three of us sadly trudged back to the cottage. I said them so fast that they seemed to run all together. "WhatamIgonnado?" My head was whirling from the dilemma we were in as I sought guidance from somewhere in the skunk fog with those words, "WhatamIgonnado?" as if the answer were soon to be delivered from above.

Kel waiting inside the cottage, said later that he could hear my voice chanting at first far away and steadily growing louder and louder as we neared the door which I threw open dramatically. B.B. charged through the open door, and plowing her way across the pretty area rug, rubbed her chin and neck on it and the lower part of the bedspread as she passed by the four-poster bed across from the cheerily burning fireplace. Before she even got to Kel, who was sitting in one of the comfortable chairs on the far side of the cottage, the wave of skunk flooded into his nostrils. I was just beginning to try and explain what had happened and why it wasn't my fault when he sprang out of his easy chair with a look on his face like an evil jack-in-the-box. He took swift action to protect the interior furnishings.

"What in the Hell do you think you're doing? Why did you let her in here? She's getting that stench all over everything!"

He plucked her leash from my left hand as quickly and easily as a pickpocket steals a wallet, grabbed me securely by my left shoulder as well as any cop ever could have, and shoved us both out the door yelling, "And stay out 'til I can think what to do! Tie B.B. to the picnic table leg and stay out there with her!"

The continuing party on the balcony must have heard Kel's shouted instructions, but not hearing clearly what he'd said, might have thought it was a domestic dispute. The wind obviously wasn't blowing their way, or they might've guessed what all the hubbub was about. One of the men responded with a catcall, "Ooooooh, you tell her, man!" Then this was followed by their raucous laughter. My feelings were hurt even though I knew Kel was right to have pushed us out.

"Yeah, what had I been thinking to have let her in that cottage?" I pondered regretfully. Bea had followed us in during the melee, her tail tucked between her legs, and with that worried look on her face she hunkered down in a corner of the room to watch the scuffle. She knew that B.B. and I were in deep doo-doo.

As my poor little stinky dog and I, in my skunk-juice-saturated jeans, sat out at the picnic table I remembered our woebegone little clean-up kit. It would again be called into service. Using our meager supplies for the tremendous cleaning job that lay ahead was like sending a three-year-old boy in to quarterback for the New England Patriots! Discouragement filled my heart, as I knew that kit would never be up to the task. Then I had visions of hundreds of dollars flying up into the sky and disappearing due to the cleaning fees and redecorating costs the innkeeper was going to charge us the next day when we had to inform him about what had

58

happened. There was no other choice than to be honest and level with him because that putrid odor would linger no matter if we'd had an army of housekeepers working the rest of the night. Even worse, we'd spoiled it from now on for people wanting to stay in the cottage with their dogs as I was sure our landlord would probably ban dogs from the premises and never let another dog set foot near that cottage. Besides, no one else, with or without dogs would ever want to rent it again since it would be polluted with the smell of skunk! I was heartbroken that our best laid romantic plans had gone up in skunk spray. Vanished was the cuddling of our girls in front of the cozy fire while sipping the wine and talking over the places we'd visited today. But most of all, my heart ached for my poor Little Sprite who seemed so sad now as she licked herself near my feet trying to remove the stink.

My mantra came back as I waited outside to see what Kel would figure out to do, but this time it had changed to, "What're-we-gonna-do?" Having utmost faith in my husband's brain power to think clearly and handle any crisis made me feel hopeful that maybe it wouldn't be as bad as my wild imagination had painted it. We might all be okay and get out of this fix yet.

Deep into my depressed reverie Kel, after considering our catastrophic situation for what seemed like hours to me but was really just a few minutes, stepped to the doorway and announced grandly, "You can come back in, but B.B. has to stay tied to the picnic table while I drive to Chesterfield for tomato juice."

Since Chesterfield is such a small town, he would need to hurry to get there before 10:00 and pray there was some kind of grocery store still open. He asked for my car keys which I promptly got and placed in his outstretched hand.

"Good luck," I said, as I racked my brain to think if there was enough gas in the car to get him to and from Chesterfield after our big journey up north. At this point I couldn't remember, so I just sent him off with, "Be careful! We'll be waiting for you."

He roared out of there, a speeding bullet flying into the night as I went inside and removed my smelly jeans and put them along with B.B.'s soaked collar in a plastic bag we'd saved from some store on the way. The smell even penetrated the bag after I tied it off, so I set it outside on the porch. I put on some clean jeans and said to Bea, "What better time than now?" as I popped the cork on that red wine pouring myself a generous glass. If I was going to be miserable waiting for the outcome of Kel's trip to town, I was going to enjoy my misery with alcohol. Bea had curled up in her bed and was snoring loudly by this time, but her sharp ears pricked up to the sound of my voice.

I hated to leave B.B. outside in the cold dark all by herself, so I put on my trusty jacket and took my wine with me to sit on the hard bench at the picnic table where she was still licking herself as she tried to recover.

Even though B.B. had only a brief time to smear her chin and neck on the rug and bedspread, she had managed to leave enough of that skunk funk to permeate the entire room. I couldn't believe that Bea could sleep in there - she must've been exhausted from the road trip. After all, she was an older dog of twelve and needed her rest. For me, breathing in the fresh air out of doors in the cold sure beat staying in the cottage.

"I'm so sorry, B.B. It'll all be okay, my Black Beauty," I whispered as we sat out at the picnic table listening to the sounds of the party on the balcony next door. It must have appeared to the revelers that I was continuing to be in exile. My thoughts turned next to the future places we'd be staying on this trip, and I worried about how we could conceal the stink. The wine brought on more thoughts about Kel.

My Scheherazade of twenty-four years had been entertaining me with his true stories of past adventures all over the U.S. or just interesting occurrences that happened during regular days around Stillwater. Anytime he'd amaze our friends with an engaging, funny, true story, I would say afterward, once their laughter and mine had subsided, "Why do you think I've kept him around so long? He keeps me entertained with all the stories he tells!" Of course, they knew I was kidding. Any observant person who gets around the two of us can easily tell how much we love each other. Yet in another way I wasn't kidding, because he is an astonishing storyteller. Some of his stories are so hilarious that I truly believe he could be a successful stand-up comedian.

It was nearing 10:30 when I saw the headlights top the small hill and pull into the dooryard. Was I ever glad to see him safely back from town after he'd roared away like a shooting star into the still night with me wondering if the car had enough gas.

Surprisingly, Kel was in a jovial mood as he stepped out of the car while I came to help him unload. "I have a story to tell you," he beamed. And with the grin on his face and those words I had heard so many times before, I knew it was going to be good and probably funny. I couldn't wait.

"You have to tell me right away!" I implored him.

So, he began to relate it to me like the master storyteller that he is while we both unloaded the tomato juice and other cleaning items.

"I blazed down the highway to Chesterfield, tires screeching, and arrived at the only grocery store that I could see in the town. Luckily, this being a Saturday night, the lights were on, and it was still open! I made it there just in the nick of time since it would've closed by 10:00 according to the sign on the door, and I got there with about seven minutes to spare, give or take a few."

"Like a pro shopper I raced through the door snagging a grocery cart on my way to find the juice aisle to buy tomato juice." We'd both heard of this mythical remedy to remove skunk odor. "I loaded up half a case of family-sized cans then made a mad dash to buy some cheap shampoo to help cut the smell."

I tried to imagine Kel making a "mad dash" as he's more inclined to take his time in the grocery store, and I'm the one who always wants to get in and out as quickly as possible.

He continued, "I quickly found room spray as well and turned to head back up to the check-out area where two teenaged girls who looked to be about eighteen or nineteen were manning the cash registers. I placed those half dozen giant cans of tomato juice on the conveyor belt nearest me along with the shampoo and room spray while one cashier stood there popping her chewing gum loudly as she began to check my groceries out.

"Every time she'd ring up an item, she'd pop her gum, which she seemed to be enjoying immensely. Then after a few seconds, she'd lift her nose in the air and sniff like a bird dog that's just discovered a trail. The other girl was observing close by standing behind the counter at her cash register even though I was the only customer in the small store. After my gum-chewing clerk had checked about half the items while sniffing several times, she stopped, turned to the other cashier, and with a questioning look, declared, 'I smell skunk. Do you smell skunk?' then popped her gum noisily and more furiously as if to emphasize what she'd just asked," Kel paused a moment to let this image sink in.

"At this point I froze in place with my hands gripping the motionless conveyor belt counter as the question echoed around the three of us in the shopper-less store, waiting to see what her answer would be. The other teenage checker stepped over to see if she could get a whiff, and upon noticing that an abundance of tomato juice, shampoo, and room spray were the only items I was buying, she simultaneously comprehended the nature of the purchases and the source of the smell. Her gaze then fell on me as she gave me a quick up-and-down-once-over while I continued my statue stance and stared straight ahead not wanting to make eye contact with her and waiting for my dubious purchases to be safely sacked out of sight. She promptly turned to my bovine-faced checker who was waiting expectantly for an answer as she chewed her cud with a vacant look in her eyes like one of the cows B.B. so loved to bark at. The knowing checker shot a look to the clueless girl, then tilted her head quickly towards the cans on the counter and back again, followed by her eyes slowly rotating the same direction. Then her eyes met the other girl's in an attempt to wordlessly and somewhat politely communicate with her cohort as if trying to say silently, 'Yeah, Einstein, I do smell skunk. Take a gander at what this guy's buying!' But she spoke not a word."

At this point in the story we both began to laugh hysterically. Leave it to my beloved Kel to find something humorous even in this dire situation. After we recovered, he went on to end the story.

"Then the Mental Giant finished checking me out still wondering where that skunk smell could be coming from and how it got into the store."

"I think that girl was actually looking for a skunk who had wandered into the store by accident. Once I'd left the store, I'm sure the Sherlock Holmes clerk who'd studied the clues filled her co-worker in on how that sudden wall of skunk came to be in the store and how she knew it by what I was buying," he finished as our laughter grew into gales. I guessed the people who were still partying on the balcony heard us and figured we made up.

We chuckled again at the absurdity of it all as we discovered to our delight that there was a hose outside our cottage which we could hook up to use on B.B. for her tomato juice bath. Poor B.B. hated being smothered in all that juice and then rinsed on that frigid night. I wasn't sure who hated it more, she or we. She kept shaking her fur trying to get the water and juice off of her which spread the droplets all over us along with the smell. The tomato juice was not the miracle cure that we'd thought it would be. It had proven to be more of an old wives' tale. We

64

opened the shampoo and used some of it to try and cut the stink. Then we rinsed her again and tried to dry her off with some of the extra towels from the cottage. But that awful odor of skunk still clung to her fur!

While letting B.B. get a little dryer with the towel wrapped around her for warmth and tied to the picnic table, we used most of our bottle of rug cleaner made especially for homes with pets from our inadequate clean-up kit to try and get the stench out of the area rug and off the bedspread where B.B. had rubbed her head and "chinned" on it. When B.B. skimmed the point of her chin along the edge of a couch or a bedspread more like a cat an activity she did quite often, we called it "chinning." Then we sprayed that room thoroughly with the bathroom aerosol we'd brought along as well as the spray Kel had purchased at the store in Chesterfield. We purged and polished that room as if the President of the United States, the Queen of England, and the Pope were all coming to pay us a visit. Thinking it smelled a little better, we could tell that the odor certainly wasn't eradicated entirely like we'd hoped it would be.

"Let's just get the pen and tarp and go ahead and put her inside the cottage by the fire," Kel said, resigning himself to the reality that this wasn't going to be an easy fix.

Both of us were as happy as two turkeys pardoned the day before Thanksgiving at our foresight and preparedness in bringing the tarp and dog pen in case of an emergency. Kel's early Boy Scout training to "Be prepared" had come through again in a pinch, for this definitely was an emergency! Once we settled B.B. aka Blackie Bea in front of the fireplace on the widely spread out tarp with the large wire pen circling her, we began to devise a plan about what to tell

65

our innkeeper the next morning before we checked out.

As usual, my creative, right-brained husband came up with a solution that was "truthy," and that we hoped would not forfeit our substantial deposit on the cottage in the process.

"We'll speak with the lady who serves the breakfast whom we met this morning and ask her if they've had many people get skunked here at their inn. Then after her answer we'll inform her that we were out walking our two dogs last night, and we all got skunked!"

It all depended on how you defined the word, "skunked," because in essence we all HAD been skunked eventually due to B.B.'s cross contamination antics. I was beginning to like this plan.

"We'll say that we washed our dogs in tomato juice and shampoo, as well as ourselves, but we just couldn't get the smell out. We truthfully can say that we're afraid some of it might've gotten into the cottage from our clothing. Then we'll warn her that whoever cleans the cottage will probably smell a little bit of skunk scent in there after we've checked out, even though we tried to be careful and clean up the cottage ourselves."

I heartily agreed with this tack of making her feel guilty about poor little us getting skunked, which had ruined our wonderful vacation. Kel added that telling her about the cleaning we did, which really had only made a dent in the skunk fumes, would remove the element of olfactory surprise in case the housekeeper got a whiff of them. I secretly crossed my fingers in hopes that our ploy would work so we could go merrily on our way to rise to the challenges that I knew lay ahead of us in the other nice places where we were booked to stay.

66

We were all so bushed by the end of this seemingly never-ending day, that as soon as our heads hit the pillows or the tarp, as the case may be, we fell into a somewhat stressful sleep with wisps of skunk in our noses and visions of upturned black and white-striped tails dancing in our heads.

Chapter 8 A Visit to The Witch Capital

We executed our skunk stink plan after eating our breakfast at the main inn building, by speaking to the lady in charge there.

She was very apologetic about the skunk problem, to our relief, as she said, "Yes, we've had some trouble with skunks in the past." So, we felt like our conversation with her had gone well. Maybe we wouldn't lose our deposit after all. My heart began to lighten until I remembered the clothing we'd had on while bathing B.B. That awful scent permeated it.

"This morning we better go wash our stinky clothes before we pack up so let's check out if there's a laundry in town," I suggested.

"Okay, I think I saw one when I went into town last night," Kel answered helpfully.

Luck was with us as we found it on their main street, and thankfully, it was open. We were nearly the only people in there doing laundry on a Sunday morning. I was grateful for that since the skunk stench was spreading throughout the big room before I could even get everything loaded into the washing machine from the plastic bags in which I had sealed them. Hurriedly I got it washing before the attendant could get a nose full of it. If she'd picked up the scent, I was afraid she wouldn't even want us putting those nasty smelling clothes and B.B.'s collar in one of their machines. "I wonder if this will even get the smell out?" I muttered to myself. Luckily, the washing removed the skunk smell from our clothing, but B.B.'s collar still retained the pungent smell. I had to seal it up in the plastic bags again.

Hurrying back to the girls who were waiting patiently for us at our cottage, we packed the car, checked out, and hit the road for the Hawthorne Hotel in Salem, Massachusetts, the ultimate place to visit in October.

The only annoying thing about the drive was having to keep all the windows rolled completely down due to the way the skunk odor still clung to B.B.'s fur. But we hoped to air her out with the fresh wind blowing through the car. Since the air whistling through was cold, we had to wear our jackets. We tried running the heater which just made the skunk fumes smell stronger. So, we shivered and suffered in silence as we made our way to Salem. Like Hansel and Gretel leaving breadcrumbs along the path, we left a scent of skunk juice behind us that even an old hunting dog with a deficient nose would've been able to follow.

We knew the Hawthorne Hotel was dog friendly, but worried that it might not be skunked-dog friendly. This skunking had definitely thrown a kink into the last half of our trip. There was no choice but to make the best of it and go on. Canceling was just not an option.

To this day we are totally in agreement with innkeepers charging a large refundable deposit for dogs. We never balked at paying it since we were 99.9% sure we'd get our deposit refunded due to our girls' good manners. Being responsible dog owners, it is our unspoken promise to

cause no harm to anyone or anything when we travel with our dogs. This is not the case with everyone, however; some people don't even pick up the dog doo. We step around it littering the grassy areas. Apparently, we left no damage at the cottage since they never contacted us again except to credit our refundable deposit back to us later. Evidently the extensive cleaning we did had worked. The skunk smell must have dissipated enough to pass inspection by the time the housekeeper arrived. After all, the clerk said they had issues with skunks before.

Upon our arrival in Salem we found the Hawthorne Hotel easily. A majestic structure, it had been built in 1925 out of red brick. The old upscale hotel was quite an imposing sight.

"Wow, look at where we're staying," I gushed.

" Yeah, that is quite the hotel. We need to get moved in quickly and then visit the House of Seven Gables first," Kel said.

I hurried through the front doors to get us checked in at the large front desk in the expansive

lobby decorated with what I guess to be antique furniture from the 1920s. Feeling like I stepped

back in time, I saw that the hotel was exactly as I dreamed it would be when we booked it.

When I reminded the clerk that we had our two dogs with us she handed me the hotel's lengthy

list of policies concerning the dos and don'ts of having dogs in the room. We had put down a

hefty refundable deposit required by the hotel with us never dreaming that we might not get it

back. As I hurriedly looked over the informative sheet, that thought came first to my mind.

Shuddering, and swallowing hard, I put my hand to it signifying that I'd read and understood it,

and would abide by their rules or risk forfeiture. It was just a chance we'd have to take. If we

had to forfeit that deposit, then so be it. Of course, we'd do our best to keep the lingering smell

from doing any damage to our room here at this wonderful historic hotel.

After getting my key and one for Kel, I spotted an elevator before going back out to the car to

get him and the girls. He already had them out for a break, so they were prepped for our run

through the grand lobby. Our nerves were on edge since we could catch a hint of skunk on B.B.

from three feet away! We hoped it was just because we knew she'd been skunked, and our noses

had been filled with the putrid stench on the way down in the car even with every window open.

Maybe other people wouldn't even notice it. I pointed out the elevator to Kel.

"I guess we can take a chance on it," he said with dread.

Quickly we made our way across the lobby with the girls in tow, Kel walking an uncannily

well-behaved Bea, and I following them, controlling B.B. who wanted to dart and sniff

70

everything and everyone in there. It was obvious that she'd adapted to her horrible smell as she was behaving in her usual manner. Their eyes grew big as saucers as they looked all around the expansive lobby at the glittering chandeliers, antique furniture, and the few people who were, thankfully not paying much attention to us. Before we could reach the elevator, a couple strolled up beating us to it, punched the button, and waited in front of the doors. Stopping in our tracks, Kel and I exchanged dismayed looks knowing there was no way we could get in that tiny space with our dog who still bore the unmistakable smell of skunk.

Kel shook his head. "We can't take the chance getting in the elevator with those people."

"I know. Guess we'll have to take the stairs," I said, motioning towards the dual staircases on either side of the magnificent lobby.

So, we abruptly turned and changed directions as if we'd seen a ghost. Our room was on the fourth floor.

"I hate to make Miss Bea climb all of those stairs," I said sympathetically.

"Maybe we'll be able to take an elevator from the second floor on up to our room. We could wait there for an empty one to come down and catch it," Kel suggested.

"Good idea," I responded as we began to ascend the grand stairway on the right.

The sound of music wafted down to us as we slogged our way up the stairs.

"How nice of this hotel to have music playing for their guests' enjoyment," I observed.

However, the sight that greeted us upon turning the corner and reaching the mezzanine was something unexpected. A wedding reception was in full swing with lovely white linen cloths

71

covering all of the tables with their lush floral centerpieces adorning them. The bride and groom, looking like the quintessential couple atop their wedding cake, and all of their elegant wedding party were in a reception line greeting their copious number of guests. Everyone shone with gracefulness, poise, and good taste. And here we were in our travel clothing - jeans, sweatshirts, and jackets - looking every bit like two raggedy scarecrows who'd escaped the cornfield with our two dogs, one making her pungent olfactory contribution to this movie-like scene of perfection. I was mortified!

There was a huge table spread with the wedding feast buffet. A fussy maitre d' was bustling about quietly directing his considerable staff, who were all dressed in formal black and white attire, to "Pour this champagne here" and "Place this dish there." We stood out like two guttersnipes who mistakenly wandered into Buckingham Palace.

"Oh, God, Kel, it's a wedding reception!" I felt compelled to state the obvious.

"Let's get to the elevators as fast as we can! Come on!" Kel whispered in a growing panic.

Of course, Bea suddenly caught the aroma of the banquet food laid out so beautifully and invitingly on the long tables. She tugged at her leash wanting to get over to it to have a taste. But Kel had a tight grip, and having already shortened the extendable leash, kept her from sampling the celebratory meal. Keeping B.B. as close to me as possible, we cleared the way to the elevators cutting a swath through part of the crowd, being careful never to brush anyone in their finery. Skirting the edge of the festive ballroom and leaving a faint skunk trail behind us, we made a swift beeline to the elevators where I pushed the button. Kel and Bea weren't far

72

behind. Neither of us dared glance over our shoulders for fear of glimpsing wedding guests with their noses upraised as they caught whiffs of a strange new odor joining the party.

But watching the arrow on the old-fashioned elevator descend through the numbers, we held our breath when the doors finally opened to reveal a blessedly empty vessel of rescue. We hastily boarded this chariot of isolation which took us up to our fourth-floor room.

"What'll we do if someone is waiting to get on this elevator when we arrive at the fourth floor?" I queried.

"We'll just have to get off and hope they don't have a very good sense of smell."

As fortune would have it, there was no one waiting to get on the elevator on our floor. Once we were safely in our room we were able to relax a little.

"I think we just dodged a bullet," Kel observed. Then we both cracked up laughing uproariously.

"I wonder if the guests at that wedding reception noticed the slight smell of skunk that must've hung in the air for a moment once we'd passed through?" I chortled through my glee.

Kel hee-hawed and added, "Yeah, and I wonder if someone has gotten on that elevator and picked up the scent by now?"

"It's actually like leaving a fart in an elevator and hurrying to get off," I added. This sent us into another spasm of laughter. Making the best of a bad situation, we couldn't help feeling a little pride in our caper.

Our room was lovely with its roaring twenties decor and furniture. I could just imagine

Gatsby and his entourage partying here in all their decadence. What bootleg liquor fetes must've happened in this old hotel! I made a silent vow to keep B.B. away from all the furniture, linens, curtains, or anything else that she might be able to rub her head or chin on. Before we could get too deep into nostalgia, we noticed the TV which broke the spell of the past and brought us back to the reality that we still had a little black dog, whom we had fondly nicknamed "Skunk," with a lingering B.O. problem.

Making sure that the towels and washcloths weren't within her reach, I quickly put her in the only space that wasn't carpeted - the tiled bathroom - and shut the door. Kel spotted the transom above the door right away, and beholding the huge windows filling one entire side of our room, began to work on opening them. We both toiled away like busy squirrels cracking nuts trying to crack those windows open, a difficult thing to do because they'd probably not been opened since the 1920s. But, with some elbow grease, we were able to push them up just a little. Next Kel stood on a chair and opened the transom so there would be a steady flow of outside air through our room. We rejoiced, hoping this would keep the room from soaking up the smell of B.B.'s fur, much like rooms that soak up the nasty smell of cigarette smoke.

Now it was time to undertake the unpacking of the car after settling the girls in our antique room with the TV on to keep them quiet. We took the elevator back down, aware of the skunk funk that amazingly still lingered lightly in its enclosed space. I spotted the carts at the front doors and, declining the offer of help from the eager bellhop, snared one to make the trip back up easier. To let that bellhop anywhere near our dog would be asking for disaster. We were able to

74

pile all our stuff onto the cart to transport it all in only one trip - a minor miracle.

Looking like the Clampetts of "Beverly Hillbillies" fame, we moved in. It took both of us pushing and pulling with all our strength to get it into the elevator. But we made it back to our room in record time, grateful that the elevator seemed a little less ripe with skunk by now.

After unpacking the immediately necessary items, I began to think more about how to keep from offending the other tourists staying in the hotel when we had to take the girls out for breaks. I studied an ancient fire escape hanging precariously outside our windows. The door leading to it was down the hallway, and I thought maybe I had a solution to our problem of getting them in and out.

"I wonder if we could take the girls in and out by using the fire escape so we could avoid the elevators and even the stairs?" I put the question to Kel. "That way we wouldn't have to disturb other people with the smell."

He looked from the fire escape to me to the girls and back to the fire escape considering my proposal. Then he suddenly made his decision, saying, "No, Miss Bea would never make it down that rickety old fire escape. I'm not even sure B.B. could negotiate it or you with your bad hip for that matter. It would be suicidal! Plus, we'd never make it back up. I'm not even sure I could climb that thing safely. And with your fear of heights, you'd never be able to handle B.B. going up OR down. And I sure couldn't handle BOTH of the girls at once. I hope we don't have a fire 'cause we're doomed if we have to use that fire escape! " he added pessimistically.

I knew he was right once I studied it more carefully and thought about what he'd said. Sadly, we resigned ourselves to the fact that we'd have to sneak the girls in and out of the hotel as best we could, using the stairs or the elevator or a combination of the two to keep them away from the hotel staff and the other tourists.

"I'm glad we're only gonna be here for one night," I said, finding the silver lining and reminding Kel. We were both a little melancholy about having to act so stealthily.

Nevertheless, we had made it to Salem in the perfect month and weren't going to let anything stop us from seeing the sights. We quickly spread the tarp across the carpet, set up the pen and put B.B. in it along with a small bowl of water. She didn't seem to mind since she'd been in it the night before. Maybe she'd accepted that this would be the way it was from now on. Bea was free to move around the room as she pleased, and she pranced around in front of B.B. as if to taunt her. We left her a bowl of water as well.

Flicking on the TV to keep the girls from hearing sounds in the hallway and barking, Kel said, "Let's go find the House of Seven Gables!"

We were able to walk right to the historic home from our hotel by following the signs along the way. Obviously, this was THE major attraction in Salem upstaged only by the witches in all incarnations and sizes which were on display everywhere you looked. Since our hotel was conveniently located in the tourist section of town, everything was handily accessible. We spotted the looming gables before we actually drew very near to the house. The high, sharply pointed gables stood out clearly with two chimneys jutting above them against the bright October sky. It was a gloriously clear day. We couldn't have designed better weather in which to take in as many sights as possible. Since the house was set right beside it, we could see the harbor.

"Let's take the tour, " I suggested. Kel agreed and we bought tickets, then got in the long line that moved quickly.

The House of Seven Gables had been built in 1668 by a sea captain from Salem who was also a merchant. His name was John Turner and his descendants occupied it for three generations. Then in 1782 the Turner family parted with the house selling it to another sea captain named Samuel Ingersoll.

Unfortunately, Captain Ingersoll, active during what was referred to as the "Great Age of Sail," died at sea. His daughter, Susanna, inherited the property. Her famous cousin was none other than the author Nathaniel Hawthorne. Inspired by his visits to his cousin's regal home, he wrote his novel, The House of the Seven Gables in 1851.

It came to be the museum when it was purchased in 1908 by a philanthropist and preservationist named Caroline Emmerton. Taking a cue from Jane Addams's Hull House she hired Joseph Everett Chandler, an architect, to restore it from its run-down state to its original beauty. Emmerton's goal was to keep the house to educate future generations about its history. Using the proceeds from the tours, she helped immigrants who were settling in Salem. Thanks to her and Mr. Chandler, the house has survived and along with it many of the original period features from the 17th and 18th centuries. Even though it is a dark gray, wooden structure looking rather ominous at first, there was a lovely garden on one side with tables and chairs where we could see the harbor. A matching gray picket fence enclosed part of the well-manicured lawn.

Nathaniel Hawthorne's birthplace home built in 1750 was transported to this area along with four additional structures. A scarlet wooden structure, it stood out against the other drably colored buildings. I couldn't help but think the scarlet color was quite appropriate. All the buildings were quite impressive.

Both of us history buffs enjoyed learning about and seeing the inside of it. Lovely autumn foliage sparkling brightly surrounded all six of the structures.

"I'm starting to get hungry since we didn't stop for lunch," I declared to Kel. "Yeah, so am I. Maybe we should walk back towards our hotel and look for a place to eat in that area." "Good idea; then we can check on the girls after we eat. They'll need to be fed," I replied, eager to find a place that might have some vegetarian offerings.

After our interesting tour and an early satisfying supper, we walked back to feed the girls and give them a break. Looking out our door we saw that the hallway was empty, so we took the girls out on the leashes and trotted to the elevators.

When the doors opened there was a couple in the first elevator. We spoke to them as we backed up a bit with the girls, "We'll just wait and catch the next one." They perhaps thought we were being so polite, and we were, but we also didn't want them to catch a whiff of B.B. We just couldn't take that chance, afraid if it offended them, they might report us, and we'd get kicked out. Luckily, when the other elevator came down from a few floors above it was vacant. We

78

boarded it and escaped to the outside with ease through one of the side doors, very happy that we could get around without having to traipse through the middle of the lobby to exit the hotel.

The girls loved being out in the cool, crisp air as twilight fell, and they picked up their pace prancing along with us. Their smiles grew bigger as they sniffed everything in their paths. Lots of people were strolling around in the area looking in the shops which were decorated for Halloween mainly emphasizing witches. It was obvious that their witch persecution of 1692 was at the heart of their tourist industry.

"This reminds me of how Fall River, Massachusetts used Lizzie Borden and the murders of her father and stepmother as the draw for tourists to visit there," I mentioned to Kel. We'd stopped in Fall River back in 1994 to see the Borden house which was a print shop at that time. We'd also visited the graveyard and her new, finer home, Maplecroft.

"Yeah, they're making the most out of their witch trials to attract the tourists to come here," he concurred.

"How ironic," I muttered. It seemed just a little bit shameful to generate so much revenue off of such horrid events of the past. But here we were partaking of the sights along with a multitude of other tourists, so I had to push those thoughts out of my mind, just like I had back in Fall River ten years before. There were stores containing Tarot cards and Ouija boards as well as all kinds of witchy items.

As we viewed and inspected an array of them in the windows of the stores, the girls sniffed their way along. They were getting quite a bit of attention from passersby who'd smile as we came closer. One young man who was dressed all in black "Goth" style with coal black hair said as he met us, "I like the black one best," referring to Black Bea.

"Thanks, "I answered, smiling as we kept on moving.

One sign stopped us cold: Haunted Footsteps Tour! 8:00 - 10:30. It was advertised as a "highly acclaimed lantern stroll" which "has been a Witch City institution since 1997." Considering that we only had this one night here, we were sold, so we purchased a couple of tickets.

Just as we finished buying our tickets, we turned to continue on and met that same young man, who was walking toward us again. Once more he spoke to us confirming, "I still like the black one the best."

"Thanks," I answered him once more. Kel and I exchanged questioning looks and chuckled as we turned toward our hotel. Luckily, he hadn't asked to pet her otherwise, he would have had a reminder of her with him for the rest of the evening.

Entering a side door again we scouted out the elevators before stealthily making our way to board one. Everyone seemed to be out exploring the town, so we were able to get an empty one on the first try. The girls were satisfied with their airing, and ready to rest. Kel and I regrouped by grabbing our jackets before heading out, this time to meet our ghost tour guide.

People were already gathering at the appointed spot when we showed up. Everyone was tittering to each other about Salem and the witches as we all waited in anticipation for our tour guide. A silence fell over the crowd as a pretty young lady with blonde hair and blue eyes strode up confidently and welcomed us all to the tour. Her all-black outfit was completed by a long, black velvet cape thrown over her shoulders and tied in a bow at the top, the lining of which was a bright purple. After a brief explanation of how many haunted places we would visit and a few safety precautions we started off following her like a flock of ducklings following their mother.

She led us to several different places, some of them homes. At each stop she told us a story. One of the first stops we made was across the street from our hotel, where the witch statue we'd seen earlier in the day when we pulled into Salem stood glaring at us next to the Witch Museum.

"How many of you looked at this statue today and thought it was a witch?" she asked. Nearly everyone raised their hands. She smiled and informed us, "That's actually a statue of Roger Conant, the founder of Salem!" We all laughed at ourselves. Kel and I felt so silly having made that mistake. It was one of the few moments of levity we had on that tour. But Conant WAS wearing a big pointed hat and a full-length cape. His hair was long like a woman's and the statue WAS standing right next to a witch museum, so what else could we think? Guilt by association.

A hush fell over us as we listened intently to the frightening tales of sea captains, murderers, unfaithful wives, jailers, sheriffs, and the earthbound spirits who haunt their homes due to the wicked deeds they had committed. The horror we expected was upon us as she related each "true" story in gory detail. Sadly, I've forgotten most of them over the years, but two stuck with me even after all this time.

The first involved the old Salem Jail. For a time, it had been the oldest correctional facility

81

existing in the U.S.A. Now the run-down prison, solidly constructed of granite, is an historical location on the route of the ghost tours where bone-chilling accounts are told about its past. As we all stood staring at the forbidding-looking jail our expert storyteller gave us a little historical perspective on it before launching into her tale about one of the spooky happenings said to have taken place there. It had been built in 1813. Essex County, where Salem is located, was in the habit of not funding the jail or sheriff's department well enough. According to a twentieth-century employee who began working there in 1986 he and his coworkers had to pay for their own badges and uniforms. He said that he no longer shared the stories with townspeople of what went on in the jail because they thought he was just making it all up. Our tour guide told us that because it hadn't been updated since 1845, there were no toilets in the cells. The prisoners had to use five- gallon buckets as their bathrooms! Then once each week they were allowed to take those buckets and empty them in the jail's meager two working toilets!

An audible gasp went out from all of us on the tour when we heard this. "Oh, my God, Kel, that's so awful!" I whispered as our leader continued with her horrendous description.

Their furnace didn't function well, so the inmates were often quite cold in the winter. The miserable place was crawling with mice, rats, cockroaches, and other assorted pests as well! The employees, too, had to exist in this same environment as the prisoners. Needless to say, the stench from the full buckets and dirty bodies was nearly unbearable. The men being housed there were boiling with constant anger below the surface due to this "cruel and unusual punishment" meted out to them while paying their debt to society. Quite often this wrath

82

bubbled up and out with the inmates becoming violent. It became commonplace for the employees to be viciously attacked. There were no security cameras to deter these assaults. More than once the guards had witnessed buckets of feces being dumped on their fellow workers! Hearing this Kel said, "Those guards needed a union for sure."

It was no wonder the inmates made so many escape attempts. How they ever kept any guards working there was a mystery to us. Our guide explained that Essex County and the sheriff were finally successfully sued by the prisoners in 1984 when they expounded on the unsanitary and unsafe living conditions in the jail. Eventually in 1991 the remaining prisoners were moved over to Middleton to a new $53 million prison. The old Salem Jail is now just a hollow shell, the perfect place for hauntings, ghost tours and vandalism by teenage boys. That was the crux of the myth our teller of tales was leading up to with her history of how the jail eventually came to be abandoned.

The story goes that several teenage boys out for a night of roaming around Salem decided to sneak into the empty place. That was not a hard thing to do as there were plenty of broken windows from previous vandals. No one really knows what went on while they were in there but the next morning a terrible discovery was made in the field near the prison. Three of the boys from the group were lying neatly in a row next to each other on their backs with their arms crossed over their chests and their eyes closed as if in a peaceful slumber. They were stone cold dead! The other boys in the group had made it out alive but would never admit to being inside the jail that night. Many of the townspeople believed that the building had to be haunted after so much misery and evil had happened in there. So, they guessed the three boys had been literally scared to death by a ghost or ghosts in the prison. But who had arranged their bodies on the lawn later? According to our guide, the crime was never solved.

A chill slithered down my back complete with goose bumps as I considered the tale she'd just finished. The last true story before we all departed and went our separate ways was about Giles Corey. He was the last "witch" to be murdered by the Puritans, who had condemned him to a long, drawn-out, torturous death based on the raving accusations of three hysterical, hormone-laden teenage girls.

Already there had been nineteen other people, mostly women, who had been found guilty and hanged for witchcraft in Salem before Corey was pressed to death in September of 1692. He was sentenced to being pressed until he either admitted to witchcraft or died. This poor man was eighty-one years old when he was forcibly taken out to the field near old Salem Jail by the sheriff and townspeople, stripped naked, then covered with a door leaving only his head sticking out above the top of it. They began to coerce him to admit that he was a witch. Six large boulders were stacked on top of the door by six strong men to start the pressing. Then every hour after that they lifted another huge boulder on top of the growing pile. Our guide emphasized to us that these were not small rocks or stones, they were immensely heavy boulders! But each time they would ask him how he pled the only two words he would utter were, "More weight." He suffered this torture for many hours with one large boulder added upon his crushed body every hour. Yet he still held out, gasping, "More weight," each time they asked him for his plea.

At one point in his ongoing suffering the governor came over and stood on the boulders looking down into Corey's bulging eyes. Giles Corey refused to scream, and he certainly did not make a guilty plea. The governor, noticing that Giles's tongue was sticking out of his mouth, took his cane and rudely shoved the sad old man's tongue back into his mouth! Amazingly, they couldn't break him. He staunchly endured the ordeal, never admitting to witchcraft. The deputies gave him three mouthfuls of bread and water during the lengthy, painful hours. Finally, after an incredible 36 hours of tremendous suffering he, struggling to whisper the words, repeated, "More weight." Cursing Sheriff Corwin and all of Salem, at long last he mercifully died on September 19, 1692.

It was said that not only did he curse Corwin, but all the sheriffs to come after him. Even to this day many of the residents of Salem feel sure that Corey's spirit has never left and still loiters around the field where he was pressed to death which is now named Howard Street Cemetery. His ghostly form is often observed before and after some tragedy occurs in Salem. Our guide added that, thankfully the witch trials which had resulted in convictions and executions ended after that one horrible year. Once the teenage girls turned their eyes towards Governor William Phips's wife the witch hunts suddenly became less popular with the majority of the people and were suspended for good.

We all stood in the field in stunned silence, contemplating all her words as she finished the last ghost story of the evening. She added one more bit of information as an epilogue. Four years passed before Sheriff Corwin unexpectedly fell dead of a heart attack. He was only thirty years of age! This certainly gave credence to the curse legend. In 1978, serving as the sheriff at that time, a man by the name of Robert Cahill was affected by a rare blood disease then suffered a heart attack and finally a stroke. The physicians who examined him couldn't find a reason for any of his ailments. Due to his health problems he was forced to take early retirement. The list goes on with all the other sheriffs who suffered health or legal problems over the many years since Corey's death.

Our weaver of tales let this last bit of disturbingly intriguing information hang in the air as it sank into our collective consciousness before she bid us all farewell saying, "This concludes our Haunted Footsteps Tour. Thank you for coming along with me and being such an attentive audience. I hope you all have a safe trip back to where you're staying. Watch out for the spirits in the night. Good night and be well." Kel gave her a generous tip since we really enjoyed all of her tales and being terrified and repulsed by them. Anyway, we felt we'd gotten more than we paid for, so we thanked her profusely.

As quickly as our feet could carry us, we made our way back to the safety and security of our hotel and the reassuring sight of our dozing girls with the TV droning. Taking them out for a quick break before going to bed was easier at that later hour as we boarded the elevator and slipped out to the sidewalk. Once we crept back up to our room, I realized how exhausted I was and slept so soundly that even after soaking up all those ghost stories I didn't have any nightmares.

Chapter 9   A Ghostly Williamsburg Orb?

The day was sparkling and sunny making us glad that we were up early. During out walk with the girls all around the area Kel snapped our photo in front of the founder of Salem, Roger Conant. Knowing that it wasn't a witch statue, I took a closer look and observed that his hat was not pointed at all, but of a more Pilgrim type with a rather flat top. Because we would have a long drive to get to Baltimore where we'd booked a budget motel for just one night our schedule didn't allow us time to visit the Salem Witch Museum. Nevertheless, we couldn't resist hiking over to the Howard Street Cemetery where Giles Corey had been pressed to death back in September of 1692.

Now that it was daylight, we wanted to get one last look at the place before leaving town. The prison was right beside it for us to inspect once more also. When the four of us arrived there, Kel sat on a granite wall by the cemetery while I took his picture with his hands curled up and his head leaning to the right as if he were a ghoul or a ghost. His pose turned out to look gruesome with the headstones and the abandoned jail in the background. Now we could leave Salem satisfied that we'd closed the chapter on all of the ghosts there.

Seeing the place in the light of day was sure not as spooky as it had been the night before, but there was a lingering feeling of malevolence that still hung about the place. "Time to go pack the car!" I exclaimed looking at my watch.

Hurriedly, we took the girls back to the hotel, and when we opened the door to our room, we were pleasantly surprised that there was no scent of skunk at all. Unless we stuck our noses right up to her fur, we couldn't smell B.B. Before we left, once we'd loaded all that stuff into the car, we closed the windows and the transom. Bravely, we even took the elevator down with other people in it when we took the girls to the waiting car. Judging by their faces as we stole furtive glances, the people riding the elevator didn't notice anything out of the ordinary. If we chose to do so, we'd be able to drive with the windows rolled up, and our deposit would be credited to my account. We were elated about how we'd all triumphed over the stinky challenge.

As we made our way through many small states, the most difficult part of the journey was when we got near to New York City, a city we dearly love and have visited numerous times.

My mother and I had spent eight weeks there in the summer of 1967 when she received a scholarship to attend a workshop in linguistics at Columbia University. We lived in a residence hall with lots of other families. Teenagers from all over the U.S. and the world became my friends. At only 14 I found it an eye-opening experience. When Daddy drove up to take us back home, one of my most pleasant memories was of riding around in his twenty-foot-long 1965 red Buick Wildcat convertible as he chauffeured my best friend, Janet, and me through Central Park and around New York City one fine summer afternoon. I developed a great love for that "Rhapsody in Blue" city that has only grown stronger with every visit.

We finally left the George Washington Bridge behind, yet we could still see the tall buildings when we gazed back across the Hudson River. Seeing that grand skyline made me want to just throw care to the wind, turn around and go back, taking a detour on our trip to stay awhile in this most thrilling city of all cities. The pull on my heart was extreme filled with my desire to go and pay my respects to the grand dame. But we had to keep on driving away, guided by Kel reading the directions aloud to me that we'd printed from our computer before we left on the trip. With a promise that we'd be back someday, we pressed on.

It had been a trying trip due to so many cars on the road. The traffic had been especially heavy coming into Baltimore, even worse than New York City. When I changed lanes with a car on my right in my blind spot, I nearly had a wreck! Failing to check the outside mirror on the passenger side before I pulled over into the right lane caused this near miss. The guy in that lane fairly close behind slowed down and honked at me, and lucky for us, we didn't trade paint. A close call, it reminded me of what Daddy had taught me instructing, " Always check the mirror carefully before changing lanes, and look over your shoulder." After barely avoiding an accident, I was a lot more careful driving in the heavy traffic the rest of the way to the motel.

"We've been in eight states today on our way, counting where we started and where we ended," I announced to Kel as we pulled into the Motel 6 after seven long hours of driving.

"Glad we're finally here." I breathed a sigh of relief, as I went into the office to claim our reserved room.

When I gave my name to the woman behind the counter, she couldn't find our reservation. But luckily, she had a room like the one I thought I'd reserved that we could stay in for the night. It was the second close call of the day.

Kel had the beginnings of one of his sinus infections so as he rested, I discovered that the Baltimore Ravens were playing the Kansas City Chiefs right here in Baltimore on Monday Night

89

Football! I admit it's strange for a retired music teacher to be such a huge professional football fan, but I have been for many years. My favorite team is the San Francisco 49ers, because that's one of my favorite cities. However, I like to watch any pro game, always rooting against Dallas no matter whom they're playing.

How I wished we could've gone to that Ravens - Chiefs game. It was a pipe dream, impossible since we were so late eating and settling in, and besides, my poor Kel was under the weather. Even though the score was tied at 10-10, I had turned it off so we could get some needed sleep. I never found out who won.

The trip to Williamsburg proved to be quick and easy, and we found The Thomas Jefferson Inn, appropriately named after one of the Founding Fathers. It was no frills, but was clean and adequate, and most important, it was dog friendly. They claimed it was "one mile from Williamsburg."

"Are you going to feel like walking to Williamsburg today?" I asked Kel, concerned that he'd felt bad the night before with a sinus infection.

"I'm much better today after that good night's rest. So, if your hip can make it, I'm game."

I estimated, "I'll be okay to walk."

Kel and I took off on foot in search of Colonial Williamsburg around noon. And we walked and walked and walked. I began to realize that Williamsburg and Colonial Williamsburg must be two different communities. It was certainly not one mile to reach Colonial Williamsburg. It was more like five miles at least by the time we finally spotted what appeared to be our

90

destination. We'd already hiked deep into Williamsburg proper by then and were about to give up when we spotted the entrance.

It was a trip back in time, just as I envisioned it would be. The workers were dressed in 1700's costumes. Buildings of all kinds and shops fit the time period. They even had clothing to rent to parents for their children to wear who wanted to spend the day pretending to be colonists. Since this represents the Revolutionary War era, a group of soldiers fired muskets. Our dogs would never have enjoyed that. It was quite amazing to take it all in as best as we could in a hurry.

But after our very long walk to get there in the first place with the addition of more strolling around the large area, my hip was hurting, and I was limping worse than usual. Kel was in a weakened state from his sinus infection, so we decided to find a better way to get back. After hopping a bus, we were dropped about a block from the motel and walked the rest of the way.

When we arrived back at the motel, the girls were ready for their break and supper. Before we left Colonial Williamsburg, we purchased tickets for a "Legends and Ghost Stories Tour" for that same night. So, there was just a limited time to spend with our Blessed Bea and Little Skunk before driving back in the car this time.

A young lady all decked out in period clothing met us at the designated spot in the village to begin the ghost tour. Visiting three homes, she told us a ghost story about each one. I'd forgotten her stories as they were not as intriguing or memorable as what we'd heard in Salem. One thing I did remember that she spoke of was about tourists snapping photos inside the last home, which was quite haunted, and capturing ghostly orbs that appeared in the photos but weren't seen by the naked eye. This concluded the tour, and anyone with a camera began to madly snap away.

Kel looked at one of his digital photos he'd just taken, and right beside the young storyteller was a perfectly round glowing orb. When he showed her the picture, she confirmed that he may have, indeed filmed a ghostly apparition floating in the air right next to her! Upon further reflection later we decided that it was most likely just a flaw in the camera since that same "orb" began to appear in other photos he took in the many other places we visited, and we were pretty certain that the "spirit" hadn't followed us on the rest of our trip. But surrounded by the visions of the past, it had been exciting that night to entertain the idea that Kel might have captured something from the beyond. Immersed in the history of this great country of ours, we had enjoyed a truly remarkable day and night.

Chapter 10   Sonny in Knoxville

As the sun was just beginning to head toward the western horizon, we arrived at the beautiful Maplehurst Inn in Knoxville, Tennessee. This Victorian mansion was white with black trim around the windows. A large, rounded, half-circle, white awning was suspended over the sturdy oak door where lantern lights hung on either side. A little porch with three steps led up to it. Three yellow mums adorned the porch where they were placed up against the short, wrought iron fence. I rang the bell next to the door whereupon our enthusiastic innkeeper, Sonny popped out to greet us as if he'd been waiting right behind the door. He probably saw us pull into the driveway because Kel hadn't even had time to get the girls out of the car for a break before he strode over to our car. When he approached it with the windows all rolled down, Bea and B.B. crowded over to the one nearest him and demanded his attention by sticking their heads out as far as their necks could reach.

"I'm Sonny, your landlord," he introduced himself as he extended his hand with that famous southern hospitality we'd always heard about. After a quick shake of Kel's hand, he marched right over to the open window where the girls were sticking their heads out.

"Aren't they cute!" He exclaimed as he reached out to pet the girls on their smooth heads. Kel and I visibly cringed and exchanged raised-eyebrows looks as we saw his hand rub across B.B.'s head and then Bea's. We hoped he wouldn't smell his hand before he washed it.

"Would you like some help with your luggage?" he kindly offered.

Kel, fearing that he'd get a whiff of skunk off of B.B. if he got too much closer or too much friendlier, said, "Oh, no, that's okay. We'll get it all in by ourselves, thanks," as he quickly took Sonny's arm to guide him away from our tail-wagging, smiling girls.

It was comical the way Kel put his arm through Sonny's as if he were escorting a lady friend. Ordinarily I would've laughed at his behavior, except that I was too worried that he might not let us stay if he found out that B.B. had been skunked a mere four days ago. I couldn't smell it on her, but I wasn't taking any chances of being turned away, thinking that we may have become too accustomed to the smell and gone "nose blind."

"We'll get our dogs and get moved in right away if that's alright with you, Sonny," I said as I

93

patted him on the back giving him a gentle, tiny push towards the entrance steps to get him moving away from our car. As touchy-feelie as we were acting, anyone watching this scene play out would think he was a long lost relative we'd found. Sonny must have been affected by our instant familiarities.

"I'm going to upgrade y'all to the penthouse," he announced proudly as he got near the entrance. "I only have one other person staying here so I'll be happy to do that, but I won't charge y'all any more than what we've already agreed upon."

When he surprised us with this bonus, I felt a pang of sheepish guilt and wondered if it was our warm friendliness that had caused him to suddenly decide to do this for us or if he'd already planned on it before we ever showed up.

"Wow! Thanks so much, Sonny," I said, surprised and very grateful. "Your inn is so Beautiful."

"That's great," Kel said at the same time.

We followed him up and up and up to the penthouse suite at the tip top of the inn while gawking at all the incredible Victorian furnishings throughout the place. The inside was even more lavish than the outside.

The penthouse had a balcony with a good-sized deck, so we instantly put the girls out in the fresh air and closed the curtained French doors, so they'd have to stay out there. The balcony had a slatted wooden fence surrounding it that neither of our well-fed girls would be able to squeeze through, and it was up so high that we knew they'd never jump down from there even if one of them - B.B. - could maybe make it over the top. Bea with her hefty, rotund body would never be able to clear the short fence, and we were reasonably sure that B.B. wouldn't try. Certain they'd be safe in that enclosure they would spend the night and most of their time out

there while we stayed in this luxurious place.

The penthouse featured a jacuzzi with mirrors encircling it under a skylight right in the center of the large bathroom. A king-sized bed was located in a cozy nook in one corner of the room, and the sunken living area had antique cherry wood furniture and custom painting prints hung on the walls. A comfortable, inviting couch sat in the middle of the room up against a wall close to the French doors. In addition, there was a big walk-in closet, a TV, and a pleasant area to sit and write at a handy desk.

Thrilled by our good fortune and the generosity of our dear landlord, I made a silent pact to make sure we left no damage to his gorgeous suite. Keeping the girls outside on the deck would avoid leaving any skunk fumes inside. When we had to give them breaks, we'd take them through on their leashes as quickly as possible and not let B.B. have the chance to rub her head and chin on anything as she was so prone to do. The rest of the time, they would be fine on the deck outside since the weather was good.

The girls were a little puzzled about why they weren't being allowed to come inside with us as they stood at the French doors and looked in with inquisitive, worried expressions on their cute faces. But they soon got over it and lay down to rest, especially once their food had been eaten and they'd drunk their fill of water from their bowl. I also placed their rarely-played-with toys out there next to their dog beds. Seeming to resign themselves to their situation, they lifted their noses to sniff all the different aromas wafting on the gentle evening breeze as their eyes glanced around at the stunning view. Kel and I stood with them on the deck to take in all the scenery, too as we watched the Tennessee River flowing silently by with the setting sun reflecting golden off of the large white bridge.

While we were moving in making trip-after-trip up and down the stairs, we noticed a parlor down the hallway and to the left which had an old upright Baldwin piano. When I asked if he'd mind if I played it later Sonny told us, "That's an old 1913 piano. You're very welcome to play it. I'd love to hear you play. I'll come in and listen."

This parlor was obviously a place where visitors could congregate to read, share stories, or listen to the music while warming themselves by the cozy fire in wintertime as they lounged on the comfortable Victorian furniture. It was a delightful place to be in any season. This bed and breakfast made us feel like we were back in Colonial Williamsburg, as it offered antique accommodations but with all the comforts of the twenty-first century and for an amazing price. We were getting the best deal of all with such a gracious landlord.

Sonny's name fit his disposition as he was quite cheerful, accommodating, and warm. We genuinely liked him. After all our things were finally in our suite, we began to wonder where we could eat. Locating Sonny downstairs, we asked him.

"We're vegetarians, so we would like to eat where we can get good choices of vegetarian dinners," Kel told him. He recommended a wonderful vegetarian restaurant that wasn't very far away. After a delicious meal we came back to get the girls out for a walk over to the site of the 1982 World's Fair.

"I wanted to take you and Jeff to that fair since it wasn't that far away from Stillwater," Kel reminded me. "But you weren't at all interested in going."

"I can't believe I was so silly about traveling back then," I responded. "I'm sure glad that I'm a lot different now."

Once we'd taken a brief look around, we promised each other that we'd come back to see more of the fairgrounds the next day before we left town, as it was getting quite dark.

The girls enjoyed their fun outing and were ready to settle down on the deck once we got back to the B & B. As soon as I tucked them in, I grabbed my Scott Joplin piano book and skipped down the stairs heading straight for the parlor. Sonny saw us and joined us there. His piano was as clunky as the one over in Cahersiveen, Ireland had been with some notes that didn't

97

play and most of the rest of them horribly out of tune. A sublime Chopin Nocturne would've sounded butchered, but it really didn't matter with Ragtime music - it fit that style. The only other guest staying in the mansion heard me playing and came in to listen as well. After performing a couple of rags only, Kel and I retired to our suite for a little TV. Another day of good fortune had been with us in finding Sonny and his grand home.

Chapter 11   Extending the Olive Branch

Being a real go-getter, Sonny was up long before I was. When I went out to walk the girls, he called a cheerful, "Hello," from the kitchen where he was busily preparing a gourmet breakfast for Kel and me.

After studying Sonny during our stay, I guessed that he is about our age, with trimmed brown hair and just a few gray spots around the edges. He has a kind face with gentle eyes and a slender, fit body. His breakfast was superb southern cooking vegetarian style, and he chatted with us while we consumed it.

Sonny wanted to interest us in maybe purchasing some stocks; we thought this a bit odd for breakfast conversation but listened without making any decisions that day.

In the jacuzzi that morning, I relaxed in luxury, and Kel enjoyed it even more than I did. After breakfast and dressing, we returned with the girls on foot to the site of the World's Fair. There stood a larger-than-life statue of Sergei Rachmaninoff. The bronze casting was made by a Russian sculptor named Victor Bokarev to pay tribute to the last public performance of this great composer/performer which had been staged at the University of Tennessee February 17, 1943.

98

The benches in a half circle around part of it were made of Tennessee marble for visitors to sit on to study the statue, meditate, or just take a rest in a peaceful setting with rhododendron and hemlock growing nearby. Upon first sight of the magnificent statue, B.B. barked at it fiercely which surprised us since it didn't resemble any hoofed animal whatsoever. But when it didn't respond and we laughed, she quieted herself right away. Bea gave B.B. a disdainful look and declined to bark, instead sniffing around at the base to see if someone had left any food crumbs there.

Fountains called "The Dancing Waters" startled us as they suddenly began their show while we were standing near them with the girls. All of us quickly dodged out of the way to prevent getting wet. Starting out with a very small jet of water, each one quickly built to a huge gushing spray from the multitude of spigots sunk into a large concrete circle. Although it was quite a lovely sight to us, it was very disconcerting to the girls, especially Bea who didn't want to get her perfectly groomed fur wet. B.B. never liked being startled by anyone or anything, so they both shied away from this large liquid display. The largest fountain near the center of the arrangement shot water up into the air for probably twenty feet. The height decreased as their placement got farther away from the center. All had been carefully designed for a delightful visual effect with white space-age looking lights just outside of the borders of the concentric circles.

Across from them was the Tennessee Amphitheater, a huge, white, surreal-looking, tent-like structure. It and the golden Sunsphere sculpture were the only original surviving structures.

Seeing them made me wish I'd taken Kel up on visiting it back when he'd suggested it.

The time had come for us to make the short hike back to the Maplehurst Inn and pack up to leave. We'd be driving over to Olive Branch, Mississippi to stay with Kel's old friends from junior and senior high school, Harley and Bobbie, at their home.

Harley had been Kel's first college dorm roommate at OSU. As we always have a good time together, we were excited to get to visit with them again. We'd seen them in April of 2004 at a surprise retirement party Kel had thrown for me to celebrate my twenty-nine years of teaching which I was about to kiss goodbye in May. It had been a huge, rowdy bash at a large banquet facility not far from our home in Stillwater. He'd invited a substantial crowd of my friends from all over the U.S., and many of them had traveled quite a ways to attend. He'd also booked Jimmy LaFave and his band from Austin, Texas to entertain us at the gathering. Kel knew Jimmy quite well, having managed his band back in the 1980s when they performed around the Stillwater area playing their cover tunes and some original Red Dirt Music.

Keeping the party a surprise, wasn't easy. Kel told me that we were going to a banquet hall to film a wedding - something we did a lot on Fridays or Saturdays. Kel would film with camera one and I would work camera two from a different perspective. That particular Friday he told me that the bride wanted me to walk in filming with my camera as a surprise for the groom. So, when we entered the hall I had it going full blast.

As I scanned the anticipatory crowd through the viewfinder, I noticed that I knew everyone at this "wedding" which I found very odd. Of course, when they all yelled, "Surprise!" I realized that Kel had gone against my wishes and given me a surprise retirement party. It was an extremely fun and successful celebration where everyone had a great time. The people who own the banquet hall said they'd never seen a party where everyone had as much fun as at ours! I was very happy that he'd done it and loved seeing all of my friends and some relatives that I hadn't seen in a long time.

Back in our Knoxville suite right before we left, I sniffed around and didn't detect any skunk smell. Overjoyed that we'd taken such precaution with Sonny's lovely place, we bid him a fond and conscience-free goodbye. Then we were on our way traveling through the South to Harley's and Bobbie's house six hours away.

Bea seemed very happy to be in the car again unaware that this would be our last night on the road. She had her big, cheerful grin spread across her face as she sat next to B.B., whose ears were splayed and sticking out to each side of her head as if she had some kind of concern. But eventually she rested her chin on the windowsill and dreamed as we clicked off the miles. As I looked at them in the rearview mirror, I said the phrase that I'd praised them with so many times, "You're the best of the best, the best in the west and all the rest, the Bestest Dogs in the Whole Wide World!"

By late afternoon we turned into Harley and Bobbie's driveway since we'd gained an hour by driving back into the Central Time Zone, a very welcome surprise. Bobbie quickly met us out there to greet and help us in with all our bags.

"After we get all your stuff in, I'll give you the official tour." she said. "Harley's flying in later today and should be home somewhere between 5:00 and 6:00 if the plane's on time. His car is parked at the airport, so we won't have to pick him up."

Bobbie liked our girls immediately and petted them, saying, "They're so cute; what kind are they?"

I gave the standard Shep Pei explanation.

We again had decided not to say anything about the skunking since we weren't able to smell the scent on B.B. unless we stuck our noses right down into her fur. We figured no one but us would do that. I did it every morning to check on how strong the odor was. It persisted.

Bobbie took us on the tour of their home and outbuildings which sat on five acres of land. We didn't walk the whole five acres, but what we did see was quite pastoral. The girls were settled into a nice room on a wonderful screened-in porch, which we thought was the perfect place for them to stay. Our friends' house wasn't fancy, but it was adequate and clean. Harley, being an architect, would be able to have it remodeled if he wanted to, as they hadn't lived there long enough to do anything with it. Bobbie's mother, who was living with them had her own quarters in the full basement which was a nice arrangement for everyone.

As we toured around the property, Bobbie began to talk politics which was something she'd never done with us before. This was a sore subject as we're at opposite ends of the political spectrum. We're quite liberal and they're extremely conservative. She seemed to bait us with a lot of what she said, complaining about the lazy, demanding public school teachers knowing full well that I had been a teacher in the public schools. They had even attended my retirement party.

102

It appalled us that she aired her racist views even using the "N" word several times to describe some of the people she didn't like and as a description of all the Democrats in Congress. In fact, she had nothing but bad comments to make about the Democrats. She got on a jag of berating the Native American tribes, with me standing there as a card-carrying Cherokee. She griped about the people on welfare who she said were worthless and just didn't want to work.

Kel had spent many fun times with her and Harley. I too had laughed and cut-up with her on visits to their home when they'd lived in Tulsa. We were both shocked and saddened that she would be this rude, crude, and belligerent since they had invited us to come and stay with them on our way home. We were at her mercy like a couple of prisoners since we were going to spend the night as their guests

Unfortunately, her mood seemed to darken and get even worse the more she railed on about all kinds of policies that the government had put into place over the last few years. This really shocked us since George W. Bush was the president. We kept mum not taking any of the bait she was throwing out and by our silence were extending the olive branch to her.

Finally, we went into the living room, where we all sat down as she offered us a beer to drink. At this point, we felt like we really needed some alcohol to take the edge off of her horrible verbal attack! After finishing my beer, I went to take care of the girls. I hated to leave Kel alone in there with her, but the girls needed their walk and supper. Coming to the end of her tirade by the time I came back in, the conversation had become a bit more civil. Maybe the beer had mellowed her out? We popped open more beers and waited for Harley to appear, and around 6:00 we heard his car pull into the driveway - a very welcome sound for sure.

Harley, one of Kel's oldest and dearest friends, and Kel had many adventures together back when they were just young teenagers in junior and senior high school in Tulsa. I'd heard Kel's many entertaining stories about their escapades. Harley was always very nice to us and was smiling broadly when he came rushing through the door that evening in a hurry to greet us.

Flying in from Chicago he'd been on an architectural design job assignment. Being a very gifted architect who had been flown all over the world by his firm, we always liked to hear him tell about the astounding situations he'd encountered while working in China or other foreign countries. Once Harley arrived, Bobbie's demeanor changed completely back into the person we'd always known and loved.

"Do you all want to go out to eat at a Mexican place?" he queried after about an hour of visiting in their comfortable living room.

"We love Mexican," Kel answered.

"The girls should be just fine in their screened-in porch room while we're gone, " I added, always mindful of our precious dogs.

"Then let's get going. I'll drive," Harley exclaimed as he stood up.

We enjoyed spicy, scrumptious, Mexican dinners and margaritas at the restaurant. The conversation was lively, and we all steered clear of politics with Bobbie behaving well the rest of the evening. Glad to be back to their house, I rushed to check on the girls and found them both curled up sleeping in their beds, totally at peace with their pleasant surroundings.

We shared stories the rest of the evening until it was time for bed. None of us wanted to stay up real late as Harley had to go to work in the morning, and we had to pack up and drive home. So, before the clock struck midnight, we all said, "Goodnight."

Before we drifted off, I asked Kel, "What got into Bobbie acting and baiting us that way?"

"I couldn't begin to tell you. She's never shown that side of herself to me before."

"Well, I don't plan to ever come here again," I stated firmly.

"I can't say as I blame you." We both went to sleep still confused, and somewhat saddened, by what had taken place that afternoon.

The next morning it was raining slightly. But we were able to load up the amazing car that held so much and get the girls in without too much trouble after we'd had a bit of breakfast. Bobbie still maintained her much better mood, thankfully. Harley had to say a quick goodbye before heading off to work, and we thanked them both for their hospitality before he left.

By the time we got to Arkansas, the rain was pouring down harder. However, as we got nearer to Oklahoma it became lighter until finally the skies were clear and blue. We rolled down the windows so the girls could have one more day of sniffing, dreaming, barking at the cows and "horsiecows," and smiling at the people in other cars.

It thrilled my heart as we pulled up into our driveway with the sun dappling down on the beautiful turning leaves of a later autumn in Oklahoma.

"Everything looks good here," I said with relief.

"Yeah, it looks like nothing has been disturbed."

"And the leaves are beginning to turn now. We'll get to enjoy another fall here at home," I smiled.

After the girls shot out of the car like two round cannonballs and began busily checking out the smells while marking their territory as they squatted and peed all over the front yard, we carried all our bags and other things into our lovely home.

It looked even lovelier to me as I thought, "Absence really does make the heart grow fonder." Bea and B.B., quite obviously elated to be back, pranced about all over the lawn. Upon letting them into their backyard, B.B. ran like the wind up and down the fence to check out any scents that were present and chastise the squirrels who might be lurking above in our large trees. Bea trotted along more slowly looking for food that might've been left there.

Near the end of unpacking the car, I found the plastic sack with B.B.'s stinky collar tied up tightly in it which still bore the smell of that New Hampshire skunk. Not even taking it in the house, ever so carefully I plucked it out of that sack by the tips of my fingers so as not to get any of the stink on me and hung it by the clasp on the branch of a small tree way across the driveway from the house. And that's where it has been to this very day, a lasting memorial to our Sweet B.B. and the skunking catastrophe which happened on this, the first in a long line of dog vacations.

TRIP 2 Westward Ho!

Chapter 1   Bea and B.B. See the Grandest Canyon

Like windswept leaves the rest of October flew by after we got home from our trip to the Northeast Kingdom. The girls settled back into their routine of walking every morning to the west of our neighborhood after breakfast then sleeping most of the day. In the late afternoons before they were fed supper, we walked in the other direction. It was a golden time. After the earlier autumn we'd experienced we were all enjoying a later one here at home. The leaves were brilliant colors in contrast to the bright blue sky, and the temperatures turned cooler at night now.

Geese flew over our house and sometimes stopped on the pond across the street for a few days before flying on south honking like clown horns as they went. Election signs popped up in yards all over Stillwater like mushrooms. We had our Kerry/Edwards signs. Halloween came and went with only one little trick-or-treater knocking at our door, so we had plenty of candy left to take along on the upcoming trip. Still bowling in two leagues, we spent Friday evenings with our son, Jeff and his girlfriend and bowled with our friends Cory and Matt on Tuesdays. Life was good even though we were quite worried about the coming election.

We had good reason to fret - the election was a disaster especially in Oklahoma the reddest state of all. John Kerry lost badly to George W. Bush, and the Republicans in our state dominated the legislative races. Our State Senator, Mike Morgan was the only winning candidate whom we knew and supported. I stopped agonizing over it because it made me too angry, maybe raising my blood pressure and heart rate to unsafe levels. There were many other things to think about and preparations to be made for our trip that would begin the day after the disappointment. The thrill of traveling again with our girls and getting out of this state to a much more enlightened area for a strong dose of liberalism helped to console me.

Our destination was San Francisco, our favorite city in California. Kel and I had flown there on many trips over the years but had yet to travel there on a dog vacation. My cousins, Jim and Rosalee live in Oakland, and on some of those trips we stayed with them at their beautiful large Tudor home.

Jim is twelve years older than me. His wife is a year younger than him. I met them for the

108

first time in 1962 when my parents and I took a trip to the Seattle World's Fair. We drove out to the west coast and making our way up Highway 1, spent a full day in San Francisco with Jim's daddy, my Uncle Johnny. Later that night we met Jim and Rosalee for dinner along with Uncle Johnny. They were engaged and being in their early twenties, had plans to travel to India where Jim would do research. I must've made a horrible impression on them that night.

My uncle had shown us the sights as we made a whirlwind tour up and down the hills all over the city. Everywhere we went I was offered a soda to drink and/or something to eat. We ate lunch in Chinatown where we had tasty food with flavors I'd never experienced before at my young age of nine. We had a short visit to see my cousin, Harold who is Johnny and my mother's nephew. He was also residing in the hilly metropolis. When he offered me a soft drink, not considering the consequences of eating and drinking anything and everything I was offered, I took him up on it. That afternoon we took in a Giants baseball game where I got away with "booing" because Uncle Johnny was doing it. I was never allowed to do that at any sporting event at home. But I booed right along with him as I watched my parents out of the corner of my eye sitting beside me in their disapproving silence. Of course, I ate all kinds of junk foods at the ballgame - hotdogs, peanuts, popcorn, candy, and drank more pop.

Our family dinner that evening was at a very upscale seafood place. Once we were seated at our linen-clothed table I ordered a bacon and tomato sandwich as it was the only item on the menu that sounded even remotely good to me. The fish didn't appeal to me at all, and just the fishy smell pervading the restaurant was causing my stomach to churn. The longer we waited for our food to be served the worse I felt. Absolutely nauseated when it finally arrived, I took one bite of half a black olive adorning the top of my sandwich and promptly leaned my head over into my mother's lap and threw up! Luckily, she had her napkin in place. I was mortified - embarrassed beyond words because I was a fresh-out-of-the-third grader trying so hard to act grown-up. To say it put a damper on the dinner for everyone else is putting it mildly. I'll never forget that night, yet I don't even remember leaving the restaurant as I was in such a fog of shame. I must've blocked that part out. My poor mother and daddy felt terrible about all of the mess as well, and I was very sorry about ruining everyone's evening. By the next morning, having cleared my upset tummy and gotten a nearly comatose sleep, I felt fine and was ready to go on to Oregon and eventually Seattle. I wouldn't have blamed my cousins if they never wanted to have anything to do with me again.

However, when I reconnected with Jim many years later in my early twenties, we became close, more like siblings than cousins. Jim like me is an only child, and I have such great love for both him and Rosalee. They enjoy going to baseball games as well as art galleries or museums. They love a good glass or five of a fine wine along with gourmet food. Always planning something fun to do, they take into consideration when we'll be visiting and give us many choices of fun activities to fill our time. They never lack for interesting stories to tell, and if you need help, they're always there for you. When I introduced Kel to them they hit if off splendidly. And as they became acquainted, the more they found in common to talk about.

110

So now in November of 2004, we were both quite excited that we'd get to visit with my dear cousins again and this time, Bea and B.B. would go along. That was the most exciting thing about traveling out there for the umpteenth time.

Two important things had been added to our traveling circus and the car puzzle since our trip to the Northeast Kingdom. One was a trailer hitch to hold a new bicycle rack so we could take our hybrids with us. We barely got it installed two days before the journey was to begin.

We also purchased a car refrigerator with both AC and DC plugs. We could use one plug in the car accessory outlet and the other in the motel room electrical socket. What a find! Keeping our food and drinks cold in this compact, sturdy fridge would be easier than dealing with messy, sloppy ice chests. It even had a handle for easy carrying and two small shelves in the door for more storage. If you knew how to pack it, the small device would sure hold a lot. Being the superb packer that I am, I was able to fit in a plentiful amount of cheeses, soft drinks, "Tofu Scrambler" salad (like egg salad but made with tofu instead of eggs), analog lunch "meats" of vegetarian ham, turkey, and beef flavors, and a variety of small fruits.

Packing the car took a little longer at first with these two new additions. We had to strap the bikes into the rack very carefully and use bungee cords stretched across from wheel-to-wheel on each one to hold it steady. The bicycle shop had shown us how to load them, but it took some practice over time to speed up the process. The" Little Refrigerator That Could," as I named it, fit nicely in the very back part of the car because we had a back window on the top half of the door that would open for easy access to it. Using the convenient handle on the top of the fridge

Kel could pull it out through that open window. There was an accessory plug in the back right close to where it sat. By late morning on that rainy Wednesday with dogs, bicycles, refrigerator, and a multitude of bags safely in and on the amazing car, we set off loaded to the gills.

"Tucumcari tonight!" I exclaimed as we pulled out of our driveway.

The relentless rain kept following us streaking the windows. That afternoon it stopped and allowed us to partially roll them down. B.B. hadn't seen or smelled the cows standing out in the soaking rain so she didn't bark at them. When she finally saw them, she let loose with all the barks she'd been saving up during the first half of the drive. Bea joined the chorus not knowing why. Kel and I laughed at them both.

We rolled into sleepy Tucumcari in the early evening having gained an hour being on Mountain Time. The Motel 6 was easy to find right off the highway.

Once everything was harvested from the car the girls got a long walk and were fed and given their bowl of water. Kel and I decided to ride our bicycles a little way to test them out and make sure they were okay, after all the rain, wind, and transport on the car at eighty miles per hour during most of the drive. They were just perfect. We only took a short ride down the main strip area.

Tucumcari is not a large town so there are few choices of restaurants. A Mexican place called Del's Family Restaurant just down the way was what we decided on having spotted it on our ride. Judging by the many cars crowded into the parking lot it seemed a logical choice. The restaurant had lots of New Mexican memorabilia and photos lining the walls along with state souvenirs for sale. We realized that Del's is quite famous in the region and vegetarians fare well.

A teacher friend named Brenda had given me a journal as a retirement gift and once I filled that one, I bought another as I'd developed that enjoyable habit. The next morning, I got Kel's free coffee from the office and surprised him by serving him in bed which pleased him mightily. By pampering him with coffee in bed that day I started a tradition that has become a little perk on all our dog vacations.

When we rode our bicycles the evening before, I was attracted to America's KIX On Route 66 Mainstreet Coffee Shop & Eatery because I had always liked the song about the famous highway. We thought it looked like the best place for a good breakfast before loading up the car and moving on to Flagstaff, Arizona. The "Mother Road" stretches from Chicago to Los Angeles passing through Illinois, Kansas, Missouri, Tulsa, Oklahoma City and other Oklahoma towns as well as Texas, New Mexico, and Arizona before ending in California.

At a very pleasant rest area in New Mexico we stopped for lunch where I tied the girls' long leashes to the picnic table legs. Bea immediately scored some food nearby. When Kel caught her yelling, "No, Bea!" she chewed it up and wolfed it down swallowing it before he could fish it out of her mouth. We hoped it wouldn't hurt her. No matter how we tied the leashes our girls seemed to find a way to tangle them. And the few times they didn't do it surprised us. The travel cloth water bowl nearly always got dumped over, but it was mostly after they had drunk their fill out of it anyway.

Our Arizona Mountain Resort A-frame cabin in Flagstaff was perfect for the four of us as

113

there was plenty of land where we could take the girls for hikes and a paved road nearby for

riding our bikes. A steep staircase led us to a loft with beds in it. Bea could only glare at the

staircase as we figured she thought it was too long and steep for her to climb. B.B. quickly ran

right up to look over the upstairs and blink down on us by peeking through the slats of the loft as

we stood in the living room below. Kel was able to eventually coax Bea to try the stairs. She

was quite proud of herself, as her big grin confirmed when she slowly and cautiously made it all

the way to the top and looked down in triumph at me as B.B. had done. Kel followed behind her

to make sure she wouldn't fall as they eased up the stairs and then accompanied her on the way

down. Flatlanders like us were impressed that we could stand on our front porch and view the

sparkling snowy peak of the mountain in the distance. In fact, there had been a lot of snow

before our arrival but most of it had melted except for a few patches where it piled up in the

deepest drifts. We chose to sleep in a bedroom downstairs so Bea wouldn't have to climb up the

114

stairs at night. We couldn't stand to be separated from our girls at bedtime on this trip or at home as they always slept in the room with us in their own comfortable dog beds. It would be no different on any of our trips. The fireplace would come in handy because the night promised to be cold. There was no TV which was more of a blessing than a problem. We'd brought books along for entertainment too. Kel and I always liked to discuss ideas, plans, people, our dogs, places, and memories, never tiring of being together talking. After I retired, we spent nearly every waking moment together. Getting to spend so much time with him and the girls in close quarters made me extremely content. Kel was anxious to try out the full kitchen. Ever since we became vegetarians in 1992 Kel had taken over the cooking. He enjoyed making succulent veggie dishes for us and had become quite wonderful at it. It only stood to reason that because his mother had always been a superior cook, he must've inherited her ability. Although my dear mother had tried to teach me, I was not the greatest cook in the world. She'd been excellent fixing delicious, nutritious meals - even canning and pickling the vegetables and fruits that Daddy grew in his huge garden every summer. I wish I was more like her, but I was always in too much of a hurry to thoroughly read the recipes so lots of times I'd mess up the dishes I tried to make. Kel had earned a merit badge for cooking over Boy Scout campfires when he was in his early teens.

"I can fix dinner here tonight if you'd like," he offered.

"I'd love that. And we can open that bottle of red wine we brought along. Would you be able to build a fire too?"

Ever the Boy Scout, Kel built a terrific fire after supper using some of the wood stacked out

115

on the front porch. That was the icing on the cake, and we cuddled the girls around it, making up

for not getting to do that when we were in the cottage in Chesterfield, New Hampshire after B.B.

got skunked. Once we loved them up for a bit in front of the cheerful fire, we each took out our

books and read awhile. As the embers burned down, we turned on the computer to listen to a

part of an NPR program. Sleep came easily.

I looked out on a sunrise so bright that it completely camouflaged the huge mountain while

highlighting the tops of the trees with golden light. I got Kel's camera and captured it in a photo.

When I took him his first cup of coffee saying, "Time to wake up, Kel," he slowly came out of

his dream state and sighed as he said, "I feel really bad like the sinus infection has come back. I

don't think it ever really went away. I'll have to see a doctor today at a walk-in clinic if we can

find one."

The sad revelation made me feel so sorry for my poor darling. We didn't even bother to get

baths. After finishing our coffee, we threw on the clothing we wore the day before and loaded

the girls up to go with us to the clinic that Kel had looked up online. Knowing we might have a

lengthy wait in the car, I managed to grab my interesting true crime book which I'd been reading

last night just before we rushed out the door.

The clinic wasn't hard to find. Kel went inside while the girls and I made ourselves

comfortable in the car to wait for him to reappear. It took three hours for him to walk out with a

prescription in hand. It WAS a sinus infection which had never cleared up from that first trip.

As we drove to Grand Canyon National Park that afternoon, I flashed back about my trip here in 1962 on our way to the Seattle World's Fair. We'd stayed at a motel with a swimming pool in Williams, Arizona. My father, who taught high school biology really wanted to spend a lot of time at the Grand Canyon, but all I could think about was getting back to that motel pool which had looked so inviting to me. Now, I look back on that long- ago day with regret about my stubbornness and the fit I threw which caused him to break off our visit early to the grandest canyon of them all so I could spend about twenty minutes in that dinky pool. It was a bad case of spoiled brattishness rising to the top and boiling over.

In all his years traveling around the country, I found it hard to believe that Kel had never been to the Grand Canyon. He'd hitchhiked in the 1970s through Arizona and all over the West with his best friend, Paul missing it somehow. That's why I had insisted that he see it on this trip. As much as Kel loves and appreciates nature and the beauty of the out-of-doors due to his experiences in the Boy Scouts when he was young, I knew he'd be thrilled by this breathtaking sight.

We made it there in record time because of my lead foot on the gas pedal. Kel, my Green Man was as amazed by the magnificent place as I knew he would be. I too was awestruck viewing it through adult eyes with the admiration of nature's majestic beauty Kel had instilled in me over our twenty-four years. The sun was shining so brilliantly that it made the rainbow of colors and geologic formations stand out even more vividly backdropped by the blue, cloudless sky. Light snow dusted the tops of the trees as we looked down on them from the edge where they clung to the steep sides. Kel shot photos and video while the girls and I took it all in. Even

117

Bea and B.B. had some sense of how enormous it was. Their eyes grew wider as their ears pricked up higher and B.B.'s tail curled tighter, then they backed up away from it. Not taking any chances on one of them falling over the side, I kept them on tight, short leashes behind the fences. Too soon we decided it was time to drive back to our cabin. The red sun glowing in the west was beginning to creep slowly towards the bottom of the horizon.

Chapter 2   The Girls Witness a Gunfight!

Kel felt much healthier the next morning so we took a short bicycle ride around the area near the cabin after walking and feeding the girls. More snow had melted, and none was covering the roads. It was fun to ride a bit to explore more of Flagstaff and since it was a Saturday there wasn't the usual amount of rush hour traffic. It also energized us.

Later, as we motored out of Flagstaff and farther west, the sun shone more intensely. I loved covering the miles across the wide-open spaces where the speed limits were high, and the traffic was low so we could make great time with little stress. As the land changed from woodsy to barren desert with cactus reaching prickly, scrawny arms towards the expansive blue sky, we noticed how the weather was mild enough for short sleeves. The girls enjoyed the smells while leaning their heads out on the edges of the windows and dreamed with smiles on their faces and their eyes closed. After Bea's neck-nuzzle signal to Kel, we stopped near Kingman, Arizona shortly to give them a break by one of the tall cacti. I made sure to keep them far enough away to avoid the needles because both were eager to sniff the sharp sentinels. I also scouted around for rattlesnakes; after all, we WERE in the desert. Luckily, there were none lurking around.

118

I was relatively sure neither Bea nor B.B. would recognize the dangerous snakes. Behind us in the distance rose the mesas, their purple hues contrasting against the beige sand dunes and the scraggly green of the sage brush sprouting amidst dried- up, gray tumble weeds. The place possessed a beauty all its own. Bea wasn't "crying wolf" since she, indeed needed to pee. Of course, once Bea marked a spot, B.B. had to mark over it. Then after Kel snapped a photo of us near an otherworldly cactus we all boarded again to drive on to our next one-night stay in the town of Barstow.

The miles clicked off speedily and easily, and we were not far from our destination when we spotted a sign saying, "Visit Calico, a Ghost Town!" We came upon another sign a little farther down the highway that had an arrow pointing towards a dirt road so I slowed down to get a better look and asked, "Would you want to take a detour to that ghost town? We could stop for a while."

"Sure!" Kel said, always ready for an unplanned adventure. He was wide-eyed shocked that I wanted to go off schedule and stop for a visit to Calico as I'm the one who wants to get to our destination as fast as possible. But after visiting the Bread and Puppet Theater barns on the way to Chesterfield on our first dog vacation, I was much more open to stopping along the way when something caught our fancy. And besides, I have always been fascinated by ghost towns.

How orange all the buildings looked as the tiny town came into view with the sun hitting them as it was sinking lower in the western sky. They were even a brighter orange than Bea's beautiful soft coat. After swiftly parking the car and locking the bicycles on the rack, we let the

119

girls jump out on their leashes to investigate all this town had to offer.

Encountering a large crowd of tourists in a big circle around a "bad guy" gunslinger and the local "sheriff" who were drawing down on each other in a reenactment of a gunfight, we stopped to watch. The girls had no idea what was about to happen so when the guns fired with several loud bangs, they both jumped straight up into the air in fright with their brows wrinkled in worry and crazed looks in their wide-opened eyes. Then they abruptly turned at the exact same time to try and run back to the car, pulling hard on their leashes. By speaking softly and caressing them we were able to calm then down right where they were as the crowd was applauding the play gunfighters. Then we hastily left that scene to see more of the buildings.

A scant distance of train track laid out in a circle with a small train sitting on it offered brief tours of the mining area in Calico.

"Do you allow dogs on the train?" I asked at the ticket window.

The older gentleman inside smiled and answered, "Ma'am, we've had dogs, cats, rabbits, lizards, birds, and even pet snakes on our train. So, yes, your dogs can ride along with you for free."

"This really IS the old West!" I thought to myself. This sounded fun, so we hustled to buy our tickets and board the train.

Kel had a good hold on Bea's leash while I escorted B.B. At first, they resisted not knowing what this contraption was, but we coaxed them and B.B. was able to jump on. Kel lifted Bea on because she was having a little trouble with the step up. When they sniffed their new

120

surroundings their raised eyebrows and wide-eyed looks showed amazement. They'd never ridden on a train before. Kel lifted each of them up onto the wooden seats by us so they could see out of the open windows.

During the ride a recorded narration explained that Calico had been a mining town since 1881. During the twelve years of prosperity there had been 500 mines producing over $20 million worth of silver. But when the silver dropped in value around 1895, the bust had begun. The miners lost interest, and packing up their belongings on mules, moved to greener pastures as they abandoned the little town which had once given them and their families such a fine living. Another sad story the narrator recounted was during the time it was flourishing there had been numerous deaths of children due to bad drinking water. There was a graveyard don close to the parking lot where many of them had been buried.

The train ride was over too quickly, and we all enjoyed it immensely. After the ride the girls' eyes were still dilated with wonder. They had been perfect little ladies as they bumped along with us on the tiny choo-choo.

"Now the girls have ridden in a car, a canoe, and on a train," I said happily. We both cackled over this.

For a ghost town, the mostly empty buildings were in pretty good condition. They'd been restored in the 1950s by Walter Knott who had bought the little burg. He restored all but five of the original buildings to look exactly as they did in the 1880s. Not long after we'd visited there, Governor Schwarzenegger declared Calico to be "California's Silver Rush Ghost Town" and a

121

State Historical Landmark.

After our ride we saw all kinds of businesses while strolling around. Since I had just retired from teaching elementary music, I posed for a photo with the girls on the front porch of the old schoolhouse, a white wooden building with gray trim that had a high bell tower capped by a pointed steeple. Right behind it on the steep mountainside was the name "CALICO" spelled out in large white boulders that we saw earlier from the road below. A building made of different colored glass bottles held together by concrete gleamed in the orange light of the setting sun as we stopped to gaze at it. Lanes General Store sat on the main street near where the gunfight had scared the girls. We laughed at The Hanks Hotel which looked awfully run down. Kel took a video of the girls and me standing in front of it as he joked, "This is Carolyn with Bea and B.B. in front of where we're staying tonight."

Bea, maybe judging by the dilapidation of the building, thought it was as good a place as any to do her business. Kel had her on the leash when she assumed the position. There was no stopping her, and unfortunately, we'd not brought any doggie doo bags from the car. So, Kel, frowning, had to wait by the steaming pile for me to go rummage through a trash can by the general store to find a plastic bag so he could clean up Bea's contribution to the town. Luckily, I found one, and he hastily cleaned it up. I had to laugh. Since she was mostly his dog and he'd been holding her leash, he had to be the responsible one to clean up after her. Usually I cleaned up after both but not this time. Muttering under his breath, he deposited the bag in a nearby trash can as we made our way towards the cemetery with the sun rushing down behind the hills in the reddening sky. We didn't let the girls go into the cemetery fearing that B.B. would decide to adorn a grave. Defacing someone's final resting place even for a moment before a clean-up could happen was not something we wanted to take a chance on. While Kel put them back into the waiting car, I walked in alone for a brief look around. The many children's graves made me kind of sad. Surrounded by a multi-colored stone wall, it was a disturbingly large graveyard for such a tiny town. At the entrance a huge wooden sign announced "Calico Cemetery" printed in rugged lettering which fit the rough and tumble life the people who had lived there.

Calico was a fun surprise out in the seemingly endless desert standing as a silent tribute to a moment in time. With the sun gone, we quickly roared on into Barstow which wasn't far away.

Chapter 3   Bowsers on the Beach

I found The Cayucos Beach Inn while looking through a magazine Kel had snagged somewhere along the way on our first dog vacation. It sounded so pleasant and dog friendly that I booked it. They checked us into our suite which turned out to be very sweet, indeed. It was uniquely designed like a small house because to the left of the entrance door it had an eight-sided shape at the front of the elongated room. There was another suite above just like it, therefore, ours was called the Lower Octagonal Suite. Looking out of the west wall windows we could see the Pacific Ocean a block away. After piling all our stuff in the living room, we rushed straight to the beach with the girls for their first ocean experience as the sun began to set.

They hit the sand sniffing the smelly seaweed and salty air, listening as the waves crashed on the shore, and watching the white foam roaring over the black rocks jutting out of the wet sand.

123

They progressively realized how near to some kind of new, enormous body of water they were as their eyes lit up and grew wider and rounder. They'd never seen anything like it before in land-locked Oklahoma or the Northeast Kingdom. Their blood began to pump faster, and their minds began to spin dream upon dream as their excitement built like the waves rushing to meet the shore as they tugged and pranced on their leashes. We let them off right away. Bursting with abundant energy B.B. started running as fast as her feet could carry her. She was fairly flying effortlessly along the water's edge while the setting sun cast its red, orange, and yellow rays on the clouds dipping down near the horizon line. She seemed not to mind getting wet in the waves that splashed up against her. She didn't even seem to notice them whatsoever. When she came zooming over to check on me, her brown eyes shining with glee, I bent down to pet her. Seeing how thrilled she was with this new- found place I gave her a new nickname: "Beach Blanket B.B."

"I can smell the skunk slightly in B.B.'s wet fur right here on the back of her neck near her new pink collar," I said, dismayed, after sticking my nose down into her wet coat.

"Really?" Kel came over to smell it for himself, sticking his nose deep into B.B.'s salty, spray-soaked fur. "I can't believe how the skunk juice just hangs on and makes the smell come back when she gets wet."

"Well, I'm not going to let it worry me too much. I just hope when we rinse her off and dry her, we won't be able to smell it." But I had my fingers crossed.

B.B. would dash one way then turn abruptly and gallop at break-neck speed in the other direction letting out her boundless energy. B.C. even began to feel frisky in the brisk sea air. She jogged a short way avoiding getting her pretty, soft fur wet. She got close to the waves, then just within their reach, darted out of the way and only got her feet damp. Our girls fell in love with the vast Pacific that Sunday evening. They had the biggest smiles on their precious faces. Kel and I smiled too. We already adored and revered the magnificent ocean after being on the coast many times, but this part of the central coast was even new to us. Feeling Bea's and B.B.'s spontaneity, pleasure, and joy made the whole experience ten times better than if just the two of us were sedately strolling along contemplating the immensity of it. So, we all fell in love with Cayucos, the perfect, tiny beach town.

125

After about thirty minutes of frolicking, playing, and bolting zigzags while Kel and I walked along laughing, enchanted by their antics, we knew we needed to head back to the suite.

"I think B.B. would stay here racing around all night if we'd let her," Kel laughed.

"Yeah, even Bea is friskier than normal," I added. "But we better think about getting them back to our place because we'll have to hose B.B. off and dry her before we let her go inside. She's pretty salty and sandy and smelly."

As Bea trotted over to where Kel was standing, he looked down at her fondly and observed, "Bea's fur isn't even wet. She won't need to be hosed down."

"I'm glad about that. One dog is enough to have to rinse and dry," I chuckled, grateful that Miss Bea, the pristine princess, had saved us the trouble.

We hated to call a halt to all the fun, but it was getting late. They scampered, leash-free, following us towards the steps leading up to the sidewalk, enjoying their freedom for as long as we could let them before we attached their leashes to their choke chains. Once we got back to our wonderful room, we let a tired Bea go in while both of us went to where there was a hose for dog washing. When I checked us in, the clerk handed me two blankets to use on the furniture in case we wanted to let the girls sit on one of the chairs, on the couch, or on the bed. This was forbidden at home and in the places we stayed. We kept it that way, not wanting them to pick up any bad habits. Their soft dog beds were good enough for them to sleep in. This place was so dog friendly that the girl in the office had supplied us with a nice fluffy towel for each of them as well as treats. The office staff kept more treats in a jar on the counter for the taking which made

126

it obvious that they truly loved to cater to people who vacationed with their pets. It was the most dog friendly place we'd stayed yet.

After we cleaned B.B. up and dried her off with her special towel we went in where Bea was already happily licking her dry fur and gave them their treats before they got their supper. This time I didn't have to coax B.B. to eat. Running on the beach had sparked her appetite and she ate every bite of her food. Bea most always ate every bite and usually even licked her bowl. She did her normal barking at B.B. as if she feared B.B. might steal her food. Bea's food never lasted long enough for B.B. to grab it even if she'd wanted to.

Kel and I drove over to the touristy town of Morro Bay about four miles south of Cayucos. Morro Rock, a massive boulder, projects up out of the ocean and can be seen for miles up and down the beach. Kel had been to Morro Bay many years before and remembered this gigantic icon, the little town's claim to fame.

Later, we took the girls outside for a break and heard deep groaning and barking. Quickly making our way over to a small pier to view the dark ocean, we all scanned the blackness for whatever was making the sounds but could never see anything. The girls enjoyed sniffing around on the small pier and pricking up their ears to listen to the calling of what we learned later were sea lions mixed with the waves as they lapped against the shore.

"The noise of the waves reminds me of traffic on the freeway," I remarked.

"That's an extremely odd comparison," Kel commented, shaking his head and smiling.

Lost in our own thoughts we silently trudged back while the weird mixture of sounds

127

continued. The girls couldn't get in their beds fast enough. Their initial trip to the beach had worn them down.

The day dawned as it usually does on the Central Coast with low fog hugging the shores and cool, damp weather. As I sat at the little table by our west windows to write in my journal, I saw young students walking to their school down the way with books in backpacks and their jackets as shields against the chilly, moist air. The gray, cloudy skies didn't bother me as I thought, "How glad I am not to be teaching anymore. It would be harder for me to go to school if I lived in this dreamy place."

Later that morning the sun broke through and burned off the clouds.

"Let's take the girls over to the beach for a romp before we ride our bicycles. That way, they'll be all tired out and sleep better while we're gone," I suggested. Kel nodded his assent.

Once they smelled the sea air and heard the crashing of the waves on the rocks as we got closer to the steps leading down to the sandy shore, they both began to tug on their leashes imploring us to hurry up and let them loose. Beach Blanket B.B. and Miss Bea hit the beach with high expectations of great fun.

B.B. discovered something more fun to do than just barking at cows, chasing rabbits or running up and down in the waves. Looking down the beach she noticed the seagulls and sand pipers walking around trying to glean bits of food from the sand particles as the waves withdrew. Seeing them at the water's edge she figured she might catch one. As she sprinted towards them her feet looked like they were motorized with electric current flowing right out of the sand and

128

up through them. We could hardly see her paws moving as they were just a blur while she chased after the elusive birds. As soon as she'd get within three feet of them, they'd spread their large wings and fly up to safety raggedly crying out to each other as they followed the shoreline. Undaunted, she turned on a dime and headed the other way with her head held high and her eyes scanning the beach always looking for the next flock to pursue. That image burned into my brain so deeply that I can still see her today: a black streak charging in hot pursuit of those evasive wings against the sparkling sunshine reflecting off the water painting everything in silvery tones. She kept at it the entire time we were on the beach never seeming to tire. The only time B.B. slowed down was when she stopped to relieve herself right in the water. I didn't even have to clean up after her; the Pacific took care of that duty. Kel and I were mightily entertained by all her activities and laughed out loud as we watched, mesmerized.

Bea, on the other hand, got frisky for a few short steps then stopped to inspect something she thought might be food. She never found anything to eat, but instead, came upon the only tree on the beach. It was not alive and growing but was a little, skinny, dead sapling that someone had just stuck in the sand and decorated with seashells hung there by brightly colored strings. The way Bea sniffed and scrutinized it we could tell that she regarded this tree as a very strange object to be in the sand. The wheels were turning in her doggy brain as if to say, "This is the weirdest thing I've seen here yet. But what good is it if you can't eat it?" She snorted her disdain after finishing her inspection. We laughed at her behavior as she was just as funny, in her own way, as B.B. chasing the birds. Naturally, they both felt compelled to pee on the seaweed that was in piles all along the shoreline.

Many people were taking advantage of the sunny weather that morning - jogging, strolling, and riding bicycles. Other dogs with their owners dotted the shore but B.B. paid no mind to them. Her entire focus was on those annoying gulls. Bea's only interest was hunting for bits of food that might be hiding under the sand like Easter eggs.

Eventually, B.B. did stop for a moment to flip over onto her back and roll in the sand. It took us by surprise, because we'd never seen her roll in anything before. We were dismayed at seeing her entire face, head, and body coated with sand. It clung to her in every crevice. Even her ears and nose had sand on the insides and her bright eyes were barely visible surrounded by the stuff. Looking like some kind of sand monster that had risen out of the dunes she began her merry chase again.

"There will sure be a major clean-up today," I said.

"Good God, I can't believe she did that." came his answer.

She'd had the best time of her life so we couldn't be angry with her. Her joyous rolling was her way of telling us, "I love this so much, I can't think of what else to do with myself. I've had such a fun time!" Seeing her happiness along with Bea's was catching, and we felt gleeful, as we kept laughing wholeheartedly.

Gathering our two delightful babies to us we took off for the steps that lead to the exit from this fairyland where we'd all had so much fun and laughter together. It took both of us quite a while to get all the sand out of B.B.'s fur. Bea stayed outside with us as if supervising the washing and drying while showing her contempt for how dirty B.B. had gotten with superior looks cast her way. Once I finally finished drying her with the large, absorbent beach towel our innkeeper had provided, she looked good as new. Her black coat shone as did her little round eyes now that the sand was all washed away. She didn't seem to mind being washed and dried. She reveled in the attention and the feel of the soft towel. It was better than when we had to bathe her in tomato juice on that cold night in New Hampshire. There was only the slightest whiff of skunk in her fur now.

With the girls safely in the suite ready for a good rest, we could get on our bikes and ride down to the main shopping area of Cayucos to take a gander at the stores. Making our way through the sleepy little village was easy as there wasn't much traffic. What a charming community. Our ride couldn't have been more than three or four miles all totaled and we found

131

ourselves back at our place within the hour.

The next morning, anxious to be entertained again by Bea's and B.B.'s cavorting, we wasted no time hustling over to the sandy dunes and seaweed-laden piece of Heaven known as the beach.

The same as yesterday, Bea and B.B. strained on their leashes as we got closer and closer to the crashing waves. As we cleared the steps leading down to the sand, we released them, B.B. spied the seagulls immediately and began her mad chase. Sometimes they teased her by letting her get within a couple of feet of them then lifted off, flying out over the water near the shoreline. She ran farther out into the whitecaps giving no thought to the salty water pelting her thick fur and sloshing up over her little black head. Even those waves covering her entire head didn't faze her. Popping back up, she continued the pursuit.

"She looks just like a little black seal," remarked Kel.

"She sure does. I hope there aren't any sharks around. They might eat her," I worried.

Another nickname was born that day: "Black Seal." She was gathering plenty of nicknames on these dog vacations. So was Bea.

"I'll keep a close eye on her and the waves so I can call her in if I spot anything that looks suspicious," Kel assured me. I knew our Black Seal would respond if Kel called her. After all, he WAS the Alpha Dog.

Miss Bea was content to walk along on her eternal search for food tidbits among the seaweed piles or in the sandcastles built by young hands the day before which were now crumbling as the tide came in around the nooks and crannies in the large rocks littering the beach. She nosed her way through the seashells that had washed up but never found the prize she so desired. Her fur, not bright orange anymore but a light tan due to aging, stayed perfectly dry. Only her little feet and white toes got wet as she so cautiously picked her way down the beach avoiding the splashing waves. Since her amused grin was displayed across her sunny face, we could tell she was having just as fine a time as B.B. We let them spend as long as possible horsing around.

Before we remembered what she'd done yesterday, B.B. rolled in the sand kicking her little legs straight up into the air as she rubbed back and forth twisting on her back, then flipping over, chinned and scooted her nose and right front side along to coat every inch of herself. She snorted wet sticky sand right out of her nostrils. The two black dots that were her eyes were barely visible - the return of the Sand Monster!

We had never ridden our bikes from one town to another, so we began our trek from Cayucos to Morro Bay with some trepidation. But it was wonderful fun. Highway 1 had a wide shoulder so, we didn't have to worry about the traffic. Drivers were even bicycle friendly and we never felt threatened or endangered. This was a long four-mile ride so once we rolled into Morro Bay and made it to the tourist shopping area along the main drag we felt like we'd really done something. Four miles was easy. After a brief sojourn we rode over to Morro Rock to get a closer look then started our trip back. As we cruised nearer to the town limits of Cayucos we stopped in front of their "Welcome to Cayucos" sign which featured a brilliant yellow sun with a white pelican, wings spread and uplifted in flight, surrounded on each side by tall trees. It was a very cool 3D sign. The hills rose up behind it in the background.

"I think this is a very creative sign," observed Kel. "Why don't you take my photo with my bicycle in front of it."

Since photos of me far outnumbered those of him, I was more than happy to preserve the memory. Kel took some pictures of a real live pair of pelicans as they swam near the rocks along the shore. He photographed many of the interesting rock formations during the ride back. I was in lots of those pictures posing with my bicycle, my cheeks flushed blood red from the energy I was expending. And I took a picture of him on his bike, a little smile playing on his lips, where another huge rock projected up over his right shoulder.

All totaled our ride that day had probably been only about ten miles if that. But to us, novice, inexperienced bicyclists, it was an epiphany. How proud we were of ourselves. But nowadays, we can hardly even feel warmed up unless we've done thirty miles.

The girls were sleeping comfortably in their blanketed beds when we crept through the door. Bea was snoring loudly which made us snicker. That awoke them and started their tails wagging followed by big yawns. We only paused a moment to pet them before running bath water. After getting cleaned up from our short ride we gave the girls a little break and decided it was their turn to jump in the car and go over to Morro Bay.

Later, the evening air felt cool and fresh with the sun just beginning its descent, still giving us enough light to take the girls over to enjoy one more frolic on the beach. As I watched them, I thought, "There are fine things that money can buy but some things are worth more than all the

134

money in the world and can never be replaced. I wouldn't trade these memories of our precious girls on this Cayucos beach for a million, billion, trillion dollars." Expressing my happiness and contentment in mere words seemed amazingly shallow.

I knew it was going to be extremely hard to say goodbye and leave this locale that had bewitched us all. But I was comforted knowing in my heart that Cayucos would draw us back again before too long.

Chapter 4   City Girls

Surprisingly, the day dawned spectacularly sunny without the usual fog. After one last short frolic on the beach with the usual chasing of birds and rooting for scraps of food, we loaded up and took off on the snaky highway to San Francisco, our favorite city in California. Before we pulled away, I booked that same suite to come back in the summer. Next time Cayucos would be our main destination, and I imagined the summer would be warmer than November.

The scenery on Highway 1 was exquisite with views of the rocky, yet forested hills disappearing into the waves along the shore. Kel and I had driven this route before, but the girls had never seen this much elevated coastline. They were sniffing for all they were worth as we motored slowly around the curves and steep cliffs of this panorama. Their eyes grew wider as they looked out over the vast ocean far below. B.B.'s expression confirmed that she was dreaming, resting her chin on the windowsill while the miles clicked leisurely by. Since there were no cows for B.B. to bark at, Bea decided it was as good a time as any to get a little shuteye since she wouldn't be trampled, and it would be quieter. She curled up in her usual position in

135

the middle of the backseat not worrying about being trampled.

When we pulled up in front of the Triton, a large attractive hotel right across from the gate to Chinatown, it was just in the nick of time before the rush hour began in earnest. The dog friendly magazine where I'd found the Cayucos Beach Inn had also described this hotel. It was close to many of the famous sights of the huge city: Chinatown, St. Mary Square, Union Square, Lombard Street (the "crookedest street" in the city), and Fisherman's Wharf. It is very dog friendly, and the price is decent. Something else we found very agreeable was that it is an eco-friendly establishment.

The bellhop swooped down upon us like a hawk on a shrew as soon as I parked our brimming car at the curb. With the bicycles hanging on the rack we looked like Okies who took a wrong turn and wound up by mistake in this cosmopolitan urban Mecca. Leaving Kel to deal with the enthusiastic, helpful man I quickly hit the doors to the expansive lobby to check in. I reminded the clerk that we had our two dogs with us. He asked their names and gave me an amused look when I answered, "Bea and B.B."

"Well, that ought to be easy to remember," he giggled. It was odd that I'd never thought about how simple their names sounded. Figuring he wouldn't really care about hearing further information, I decided to forego the explanation of how they got their names.

When I came out with our keys, Kel was staving off the guy from unloading everything through the back window with the bicycles still securely in the rack on the car. In the first place, that would have been impossible, but it also would cause a lot of upset for the girls in the routine. Kel was overwrought when I approached as he was trying to get the bicycles unloaded as quickly as he could. If they were removed, we'd be able to take out the pieces of the car puzzle in the correct order through the back door as well as through all the other doors. There were things tucked in every single bit of space throughout the car.

"I'm going to have to take the girls up to the room right now," I announced. Kel's face was aghast since it would mean I was leaving him alone again with that eager bellhop.

"Well, hurry back and help me get all this stuff corralled. I don't know how much longer I can keep him from unloading everything onto the sidewalk," he whispered loudly trying to speak above the traffic noises of the city, but also trying not to let our "helper" hear. Of course, the bellhop's job and main agenda was to get the car unloaded and cleared pronto from out in front of the hotel. I nodded as I put the girls on their leashes and let them hop out safely on the right side of the car instead of the usual left because it bordered the teeming street.

As I guided the girls through the stunningly decorated lobby of the grand hotel, we found the elevator to get to our room. After our nice large two-room suite at the Cayucos Beach Inn, this room seemed even more diminutive, but nevertheless, I was glad to get into it and give the girls their water in the travel bowl before heading back down to fight the unloading war with the impatient bellboy. Though small, it was decorated in very hip furnishings which appealed to me. The whole place had a rock music theme about it.

Back at the car I saw that Kel was in a panicked frenzy with our bags, backpack, fruit basket, luggage, dog beds, dog toys, pen, tarp, refrigerator, and bicycles plus a multitude of smaller loose items all spread out like a sidewalk sale as people threaded their way through trying to get past this plethora of stuff. I was embarrassed at how shabby our things looked sitting there for all the city dwellers hurrying by to contemplate. I stood there in the midst of it all feeling like Ma Kettle.

"I can't control him," Kel whispered for my ears only, his eyes darting from the bellhop to the mishmash.

"Well, you should've been firm with him and told him not to touch anything until I came back," I shrieked in a stage whisper.

"He won't listen to me. He's in a terrible hurry to unload and get all our things up to the room on a cart."

"Ok, I'll have to manhandle him," I retorted sarcastically.

I took charge as if directing my fifth graders in a musical. At my authoritative direction the bellhop and Kel steered our bicycles into the lobby first where they were promptly put into a storage room near the front desk. This room was mostly used to store tourists' luggage so they could sightsee after they checked out but before they were due to catch their flight. It was kind of the hotel clerk to provide this perfect arrangement for our bikes since our room was so small that storing them in there would crowd us even more.

While they were accomplishing this task, I hurried to load as many of our items onto the cart that the gung-ho man had rolled out and left by all our possessions blocking the path on the sidewalk. Quickly, I was able to load about half of it by hanging some off the hooks and then piling some on the base of the cart in a rather haphazard stack.

When they returned after stowing the bikes, seeing that only half of our things were secured on the first cart, the tip-motivated guy dashed inside to retrieve a second cart to carry the rest of our hodge-podge. Kel was sweating but calming down now. I was in control as we all three hurried to fill up the second cart. Since we were able to get all the odds and ends aboard the carts, we only had to make one trip. Another employee of the hotel strode out when he saw that we were going to transport them upstairs to our room. He was the valet who would park our car in their lot somewhere unbeknownst to us which the hotel kept as a deep, dark secret. Reluctantly, I surrendered the keys knowing that from now on we'd have to ask for the car before we could make any trips. But at least we were going to be able to get everything into our room and not have to worry about making lots of trips up and down the elevators to finish the task.

The anxious bellboy commandeered one cart while Kel and I handled the other. Both carts wouldn't fit into one elevator comfortably with us inside, so we had to use both. Thankfully, we made the trip up fairly easily and got all the things into our room without too much fuss. Kel handed the bellboy a generous tip for which he thanked him profusely. Now that the unloading debacle was over, we both breathed a sigh of relief. I set about unpacking a few of the necessary items which included the girls' food, and they gobbled it down at rapid speed once Bea had done her obligatory barking at B.B.

At check-in the clerk had invited us to partake of the complimentary wine served in the lobby from 5:00 to 7:00. After what we'd just been through, we needed a drink. But we found

139

the humor in it and had to laugh about how we felt like hillbillies with all our stuff exposed for everyone walking by to evaluate. It was lucky no one had tried to steal anything as they passed by. Maybe it hadn't looked worth stealing. Kel had kept a watchful eye on it all, aware that there might've been opportunists around.

"Let's go down and have some free wine in the lobby before we take the girls out for their walk," I suggested.

"I need a drink," Kel agreed, relief flooding his face now that we'd survived the curb ordeal.

We each had a glass of California red with a few other tourists who'd taken the hotel up on their generous offer. In fact, we managed to down two glasses each before we went back up to get the girls. The wine made us feel so much better and smoothed out our nerves. What a great hotel. Free wine!

When all four of us exited the elevator doors and trotted through the lobby the attentive desk clerk who'd checked us in shouted out loudly for all to hear, "It's Bea and B.B.!" as if he were announcing them at a debutante's coming out ball or like they were contestants on a TV game show. Everyone turned to look at our girls as we quickly scurried across the few remaining feet of the lobby. Kel and I split our sides laughing at that once we were clear of the building and the doorman who, with a professional flourish, flung open the door for our departure. This was obviously a dog friendly hotel extraordinaire.

I'd asked at the front desk about a good green space where we could walk our little sweeties so they could do their business, and the clerk recommended a small park a short walk from the

140

hotel. He gave me some quick directions to St. Mary Square as I paid close attention.

The vibrant city excited the girls, especially B.B. She tugged and pulled on her leash wanting to sniff in every corner of each doorway as she moved helter-skelter while we made our way over to the park. She tried to enter the businesses we were passing by and looked at me with a question in her bright, round eyes with raised eyebrows, asking, "I just came out from a very nice, large place, so why am I not allowed in all of these smaller, lesser ones?"

"B.B.'s trying to go in every door," I laughed, pointing out her attempt for Kel to observe at the next door we came to. We both laughed and kept on going.

Bea was intrigued by every smell of food from the many diners, restaurants, and bars we went by. Her nose was held high as her big brown eyes grew wider with each new and tempting aroma that wafted on the evening air.

There was plenty to cause an overload of the senses along the way for humans as well as dogs. We had to steer the girls through the swarms of people packing the sidewalk with the bright lights of the signs flashing every color of the rainbow marking all the establishments as they lit the scenes playing out down those long city blocks. Horns blared, engines of the big buses roared mixed with the car engines; sirens wailed in the distance and drew nearer with their shrill sound only to grow softer as they fade away, the farther on they went. We were lucky that the girls weren't howlers, or they would've raised a huge ruckus in response. People speaking, coughing, or laughing and sometimes music filled the air which smelled of bus fumes, food, and tinged with a garbage or urine smell every-so-often all jumbled up together. After being in a

141

small beach town it was invigorating to us all and seemed even more alive and "big city" than ever.

We hadn't gone far when Kel had to stop while Bea assumed the position right on the sidewalk clearing a swath on either side of herself as the hectic crowd noticed her hunched stance and split around her like the parting of the Red Sea. I hastily handed Kel a dog bag. He was not happy at all about where Bea had chosen to do her business instead of waiting for the park. I said, snickering, "When you gotta go, you gotta go." I couldn't help but poke a little fun, as I thought of the many times I had walked both girls and picked up after them. Again, Kel was literally getting a feel of what it was like picking up after "his dog." Fortunately, he found a trashcan at the next corner so he could dispose of the stinky bag. I was glad that B.B. was able to wait until we got into St. Mary Square Park before she did her evening business. It was easily cleaned up and disposed of as well in the park's handy trashcan.

St. Mary Square Park was the perfect place for us to walk around in. Bea did her usual surveying for dropped food, but the pigeons had beaten her to it. There wasn't a crumb to be found. B.B. wanted to chase the pigeons like she'd done the seagulls on the beach, but we weren't about to let her off her leash in this huge metropolis. She did run at them while on her twelve-foot leash but couldn't get near them. Still, she was delighted at making them fly up in a flurry to get away as her sparkling eyes and big smile revealed. The tiny patch of greenery and some good-sized trees ensured our brief enjoyment of the park before making our way back to our hotel.

142

Once we got into the room, I gave Cousin Jim a call. He was exuberant as always and made a date to meet us for the next evening at an all vegetarian restaurant in Palo Alto not far from the Bay Area. We were thrilled that Rosalee would be with him too. Since they are all about good food and wine, we never doubted that this place would be terrific. Always having lots of laughs, interesting conversation and elegant food and drink when we got together, we looked forward to it. With not a care in the world, I was excited to be back in this wonderful heart-throbbing city.

Chapter 5 Jim and Rosalee

Pouring rain greeted us the next day, November 11th, Veterans Day. If any parades were planned to honor those who'd served, the participants were going to get wet. The girls still had to have their walk down to St. Mary Square so we put on our hooded ponchos, thankful that we'd remembered to bring them along, and hustled the girls down the sidewalk as quickly as we could while trying to stay under the business awnings. Bea didn't want to get her furry coat wet, but she and B.B. needed to do their business, and we hoped that Bea would be able to wait 'til we got to the park this time.

People were huddling under their umbrellas or wearing raincoats as they sped down the sidewalk. We dodged our way past them until we were in the pretty park where both girls accomplished, in record time what we'd set out to do. Once we cleaned up after our respective dogs, we wasted no time in hotfooting it back to the warm, dry shelter of our nice hotel.

As noon was nearing, we sought out a tiny vegetarian restaurant where we'd eaten several times before. It is called Lucky Creation and has seating for only about a dozen people if they

143

share a table with strangers. The place mostly does "take out" but we always like to sit in there to eat. The way they prepare their faux meats makes us swear that we are eating the real thing. The first time we discovered the little diner we kept checking with the waitress to make sure it was NOT real meat, and she kept assuring us that it was NOT. They offer every kind of analog meat you could want - beef, chicken, pork, duck, and fish. Their tasty dishes always amaze us. We'd be sampling a new-to-us vegetarian restaurant tonight with Jim and Rosalee and comparing it to this one.

They both had gone to the University of California, Berkeley where they'd met while doing a work shift in the co-op dorm kitchen. He's an incredible linguist who speaks several different languages fluently which comes in handy as they travel all over the world to places Kel and I would never even think of going. He and Rosalee were married "too young," as she says, in 1962 when he was 21 and she was just 20. In June of 1966 their daughter, Greta, was born. They lived in India for two more years where Jim did his PhD research on Gondi, a tribal Dravidian language. In order to stretch a one-year grant into two Jim took a job working for six months at the Language Office for the Peace Corps in 1968. Then he finished his PhD work at the University of Pennsylvania. Once they'd moved back to the Bay Area, Rosalee got her Master's in social work at San Francisco State. Jim worked at his Alma Mater, Berkeley, in the department of South Asia Studies until 1974 when it was eliminated due to the recession of the mid - 1970s. He looked unsuccessfully for a new job in his field of study, but found he had a knack for the real estate business. When he took care of the acquisition of their first home,

144

he discovered how much he enjoyed buying and selling houses. Rosalee, after working as the Intensive Care Nursery social worker at Kaiser Hospital, became interested in people with developmental disabilities and toiled at several social work jobs until founding her own agency in 1994 for adults with developmental disabilities who desired to live independently.

Happy-Go-Lucky Jim loves living life to the fullest, a very good quality. He's nearly always smiling, never in a hurry, and willing to sample food or drink without giving a thought to calories or political correctness. Being an avid movie fan, he and Kel always have much to visit about with regards to the newest films as Kel is a video critic who writes a review column under a pen name for a monthly regional newspaper.

One of the funniest things I've ever experienced happened when Jim and Rosalee joined us in Eureka Springs, Arkansas, back in the 1990s. Having traveled there for a great many trips, we had made a lot of friends, all of them vegetarians or vegans. An artistic crowd, most of us embrace the same liberal political views. We all gathered for lunch at a trendy restaurant which offered both meat and vegetarian fare. I introduced my cousins to our friends who were there to share the noontime meal with us. When it came time to order, Jim, with a babe's innocence, spoke out loudly in that big wonderful voice of his saying, "I'll have the veal."

You could've heard a pin drop for a split second at that table of eight then the collective gasp as all heads turned craning their necks slowly to inspect this man more thoroughly after the initial shock of hearing what he ordered. The smile on his face confirmed that he had no idea why anyone would be upset by his choice. In fact, he didn't even seem to notice that everyone but Kel and I was staring at him. After seeing his smiling face, the two of us began looking down not making any eye contact with each other as we were trying not to laugh since we know him so well. This was very typical behavior and it didn't really surprise us. We knew he wasn't trying to offend any of us, so it just endeared him to us more. After all, he just wanted what looked good to him with no concept of the political climate at that table.

However, Rosalee is another matter. Knowing full well about how veal calves are torn from their mothers when they can barely stand and kept in tiny slotted pens for months where they can't even turn around before they're slaughtered while still quite young, she was chagrined that he ordered veal in front of all these animal rights vegetarians and vegans. Her face turned bright red for her guilt-free husband.

She confided to Kel and me later, "I was hoping he'd order the fish."

The three of us had a secretive laugh about the complete guilelessness of my dear cousin. He truly was unaware that veal was probably the worst possible dish anyone could order considering the crowd who was in attendance. I believe Rosalee, in empathy, ordered a vegetarian dish.

The epitome of the Earth Mother, she is nurturing, kind, calm. and soft-spoken, with grounded looks and an aura about her that make you feel at home, welcome and relaxed right away as if you've known her all your life. It was no wonder she went into social work because she loves people, gives them the benefit of the doubt and is quite intuitive picking up on their needs, wants, likes and dislikes with an astonishing quickness. She never gets in a hurry, and

146

now, as a retired social worker, Rosalee seems to always know how to deal with any situation that arises. Just like her husband, she lives life to the fullest. She read Kel and me as easily as a good book and was intuitive enough to know what we enjoy doing after spending just a short time visiting with us on our numerous trips to the Bay Area. One time she loaned us her old Volvo and suggested we drive to the amusement park in Santa Cruz for the day. It was ideal for a fun day trip and exactly what we wanted to do. Our love for my cousins grew more every time we got together, and we anticipated a wonderful evening that was about to begin.

I had to call the front desk to request that our car be brought around. The man said it would be in front of the hotel in ten minutes. We decided we should take the girls along and let them sleep in the car while we ate and visited. That way we could give them a break before driving back to the city. We were afraid to leave them in for as long as we might be gone. Jim and Rosalee wouldn't be in any hurry, and to be truthful, neither would Kel. I was always the one who had to move things along. But I didn't want to rush through the dinner or the visiting during and after desiring to savor every bite, sip, and word with them.

As we came through the fashionable lobby the Johnny-on-the-spot doorman threw open the door for B.B. and me as we were a little ahead of Kel and Bea. Unfortunately, the car valet was just entering that very same door and met us head-on which took B.B. by surprise. Now B.B. never liked to be surprised, especially by a man in a uniform wearing a little square odd-looking hat, so she began to snarl and bark furiously at him. I tightened up pronto on her leash, scolded her, and dragged her by him all the while apologizing for her terrible behavior trying to explain to him that she didn't like to be surprised. Hearing the commotion, Kel came hurrying up to see what had happened towing Bea along behind him. The rattled man handed me the key to the car as Kel gave him a nicer-than-usual tip to make up for B.B.'s unexpected outburst. There was a glut of traffic in the street so Kel rapidly opened the door nearest the sidewalk for safety. Then the girls sprang in right on cue.

Looking forward to visiting with Jim and Rosalee, we rapidly drove over to Palo Alto. It was a lovely evening now that the rain had moved to the east, and the sun even made a brief appearance before it began to sink in the west. The traffic was not too bad in the direction we were heading. The big tie-up had been for people commuting over from San Francisco to Oakland across the Bay Bridge. It was only a little over thirty miles to the home of Stanford University, a place Kel and I had never been before. We'd certainly heard of Stanford and were excited to get to see the town where it was located. The drive over was not bad at all, even rather pleasant, and the girls were happy to get to go along as their smiles showed how much they enjoyed the smells along the way.

We had a magnificent vegetarian dinner accompanied by some fine wines as Jim's a connoisseur and knows how to pick just the right vintages and flavors to complement the meal.

It was as if we hadn't been away from them for the years between our last visit and this one. Time hadn't changed them, and the great fondness was warm and abundant between the four of us. They were in mourning over the sad election even more so than we were. We discussed that and so many other things as we got caught up on what their and our lives had been like since

we'd last seen them nearly ten years previous. Before we parted for the night, they invited us to

come over to their big house in Oakland for the traditional family dinner that they would always

have for us once we started making it a habit to visit every few years. At that time, we'd get to

visit with their two daughters, their husbands, and children. It was always a heartwarming

reunion.

Since Kel and I are only children, we longed for these big family reunions like we'd had in the

past when our parents and their siblings had gathered to celebrate on holidays. That generation

is gone now, and our relatives who are left either aren't our close friends or aren't living close

enough for us to be invited very often to their homes. This family reunion promised to be a real

blast, and we were quite elated that we'd be able to get our family fix with Jim and Rosalee's

large, delightful clan. But best of all, the girls were invited too.

Chapter 6 Bea's New Nickname

It was not raining when we awoke and took the girls out for their necessary walk to good ol' St. Mary Square. Quite pleased about the weather, we hadn't gone far when Bea hunched over and pooped right on the sidewalk like she had when we first walked them on the streets of San Francisco. She grinned up at Kel who was mortified that she hadn't waited. Her eyes peered at him as if saying, "Well, I've left you another treasure. Aren't you going to pick it up?" I quickly handed him a dog bag, and he just as quickly scooped it up, tied it off, and deposited it at the same trashcan as the first day we were here. He was getting quite familiar with that particular can. Nobody acted as if they noticed.

Just a short distance from the park Bea pulled up again to a tiny green spot bordering the sidewalk, and this time she let go a stream of diarrhea with her eyes again signaling him that it was there for the taking.

"Oh, God, Bea has the squirts!" he wailed.

" I see that. I sure hope she can get over them since we're bicycling today."

"Yeah, let's hope she gets it all out of her system."

"I wonder what gave her that?" I puzzled. "It could've been something she ate on the sly when we didn't catch her," Kel reasoned.

"I bet you're right. She loves to sneak food. and might've eaten something that was spoiled."

Before Bea made another soupy mess, we were able to proceed into the park and pick out an out-of-the-way patch of green.

"Miss Bea has become a Shitting Machine!" Kel exclaimed. I had to laugh since it was true. She always seemed able to squeeze out something when we walked them anywhere. And now that her tummy was upset, she was really leaving a trail behind. We were both worried about her but not enough to stop us from laughing about her new nickname.

B.B. lunged at the pigeons in the park for a short spell then relieved herself. There were many times when B.B. didn't need to go, and Bea went enough for both of them. Before we left the park, the Shitting Machine went again, and it was all liquid. We stayed and lollygagged longer than usual giving Bea plenty of time to get it all out of her system, we hoped. Each time she pooped she looked up at Kel with her eyebrows raised in an expectant expression. She seemed very proud of herself because she'd given so much of what her daddy had apparently wanted as he usually was quick to get it in the bag. She still had a huge, panting smile on her face even when Kel couldn't bag what she was putting out.

"Let's take our Shitting Machine back to the hotel and hope for the best," I said as we turned to leave the park.

Thankfully, Bea didn't need to stop any more all the way back. It seemed she'd gotten it all out now. But to be safe, we decided to take the girls along with us when we drove over to the Presidio for our bicycle ride. They could sleep in the car with the windows cracked open a bit, and we could check on them after a shorter length of time instead of leaving them in the room and risking a bad accident. Even with the sun out the day was quite cool, so they'd be in no danger from overheating in the car. We figured if she messed in there, we could clean it up with our handy clean-up-kit. It would be easier than setting up the pen and tarp for her to be confined in, and besides, the room was too small to even set it up, although we discussed doing that.

I phoned for the car and the bicycles. We grabbed our helmets and gear and the girls' leashes as we hustled down about ten minutes later. Sure enough, just as we burst out of the hotel entrance door hurled open by the exuberant doorman, the car valet met us on the sidewalk with the keys in his hand. B.B. promptly began to snarl and bark at him even though he hadn't surprised her this time. Remembering how he'd surprised her the evening before, she had taken a dislike to him and couldn't shake it off. Again, I scolded her and apologized to him while Kel dutifully handed him another very nice tip. We speedily let the girls leap into the backseat from the right side where they'd be safe from all the busy traffic in the street. Then we strapped the bicycles into the handy rack. Having done it now for so many times on this trip, we'd gotten pretty adept at loading them.

After driving to Golden Gate Park, I was able to find a nice, shady parking place so the girls could have a comfortable sleep while we rode. Just in case the Shitting Machine had to go again, we took them out for a very quick break in the beautiful greenery. We were both heartened when she didn't do a thing except sniff around for food under the trees while B.B. looked for pigeons to scare.   "I think she got it all out," Kel said happily.

We got them back into the car, rolled each window down just a tad and removed our bicycles from the sturdy rack. After landmarking exactly where we were parked, I locked the car

152

as the girls looked out at me blinking their sleepy eyes. Then we rode away towards the Presidio and Golden Gate Park wondering what kind of bicycling adventure this large hilly city would hold for us.

After riding awhile, we got off our bicycles to walk out on the beach where the Golden Gate Bridge rose up in all its majestic rosiness behind us. We posed in turn with our bikes while one of us snapped the photo, so we'd always remember how blue the ocean was and how happy we were with that incredible icon in the distance connecting our beloved city with Sausalito to the north. It seemed like we'd ridden miles and miles when it was time to make our way back to the girls and hope that we'd find them sleeping peacefully with no mess to clean up.

Relief flooded over us seeing them sound asleep in their normal traveling position in the middle of the backseat with B.B.'s head resting in the middle of Bea's back. As soon as they heard us, they woke up and while Kel loaded the bicycles on the rack, I put their leashes on and gave them a good break in the park again.

Kel had researched dog parks and located one not far from where we were after what had seemed like a lengthy ride.

"We could lock the bicycles on the car and let the girls run around a bit in a dog park that's close by here that I found on the Internet," he said testing the waters with me.

"That's a great idea. They've never been to a dog park. They'll have so much fun with the other dogs," I trilled imagining how they'd play and roughhouse with the multitude of dogs who were probably romping in the park at this very moment.

153

Soon we arrived there and took the girls into it on their leashes. Once they were safely through the double-gated entry, we removed their leashes but kept their choke chains on just in case we needed to leash them up again quickly. We didn't know how they might react to being in with a whole lot of unfamiliar dogs and we sure didn't want any trouble.

It was a huge park with wonderful large trees and soft green grass. There were long, green benches for the owners to sit on to observe their dogs while they romped and cavorted around. All of them were joyfully running free. We wanted that for our girls too. Kel and I sat down on a bench in the shade of one of the inviting trees. Bea and B.B. stood staring at the dogs scattered all over the park who were amusing themselves with their new doggy friends. However, our girls were frozen with bewilderment it seemed. B.B. turned her back on all of the happy canines and sauntered closer to us with a confused look on her face that said, "Why did you bring us to this place full of dogs? What could you be thinking putting us in here with a bunch of dogs? Are you crazy? We don't belong in here with all these dogs!" She was having nothing to do with any of her species. Bea just stood out a short distance from us and stared at all the excited pups enjoying each other and their wonderful freedom from leashes.

Suddenly, B.B. took off at a dead run towards a professional dog walker who'd just entered through the double-gate with five dogs of all sizes, ages, and breeds still on leashes. She paid no attention whatsoever to the young woman's charges, but instead, stopped right beside her looking up asking to be petted. After releasing her pack, the kind, young lady bent down, patted B.B. on her head and scratched her behind the ears which made B.B.'s curly tail coil tighter as she

154

wagged it furiously. Her open-mouth smile grew larger as she locked eyes with the benevolent woman. It was obvious she was quite pleased with herself for getting some positive feedback from one of the humans in the park. Bea's face had that wrinkled brows worried look all over it as she stood transfixed with her left front paw raised slightly as if she were about to point or take a step but just couldn't bring herself to do it. She seemed to be saying, "There is no way I'm going to get near to any of those dogs!" As the other dogs scampered happily around, she remained aloof just watching with a disapproving look on her expressive face. Then very slowly she wandered back to us sniffing as she went to see if there were any particles of food hiding in the sparse grass.

After being caressed by the friendly dog walker, B.B. shot back across the wide expansive park to where we were sitting on the bench and splitting our sides laughing at the way our girls were spending their leash-free time here. Upon being back near us, she immediately began to sniff around where other dogs had peed, as their scents drew pictures of them in her brain. We chalked up the visit there as entertainment for us. The girls had sure made us laugh with their standoffishness. We hadn't laughed that hard for quite some time. This episode was funnier than when Kel had coined Bea's new nickname earlier in the day. After about thirty minutes we left. Stunned by their behavior, it had sure been an eye-opening experience for us, and we wondered if they would react differently the next time?

Once we unloaded the girls, the bicycles, and all our gear, we turned the car over to the valet while B.B. barked at him again a for good measure, and I apologized profusely as Kel tipped him well. We took our little sweeties up to our room where I fed them after which they curled up in their beds exhausted from ignoring all those dogs. Kel and I cleaned up rapidly, so we'd be able to drive over to Berkeley and eat at Intermezzo, a wonderful hangout on Telegraph Avenue that serves giant salads and sandwiches. We always made a point to sit in the window and watch the interesting freaky folks going by along the busy sidewalk. Fitting into the liberal, tolerant atmosphere of Berkeley much more than where we lived back in Oklahoma, we felt right at home. There was no comparison between these two college towns. Berkeley is a real university town whereas Stillwater is a small town that happens to have a college located in it. Even though Kel has long, naturally curly, Afro style hair and wears cool, trendy clothes, and I look like a younger-than-my-real-age "hippie gypsy" wearing my sizable amount of jewelry, hip clothing, and sporting my long, straight, Native American locks, we didn't even turn any heads in Berkeley like we do sometimes in Stillwater. That was the way one of my 5th grade music students, Duncan, had described me to his mother, when he told her one day, "She looks like a hippie gypsy." Once when I ran into her shopping, she'd revealed this to me now that he'd grown up and was in college. He was always a bright student, and I thought it a very observant, astute description for such a young boy.

Since the Shitting Machine had turned off, we decided to let the girls stay in the room and sleep. It was so much easier to get the car out again without all the aggressive behavior B.B. had been heaping on the unfortunate valet. Because we'd just taken it out less than two hours before, Kel didn't give the man a tip at all this time. I just grabbed the keys from him rapidly and we

156

buzzed off with a "Thanks," thrown over my shoulder.

Having satisfied ourselves that Berkeley was still relatively freaky and left wing by observing the amazing throng of people going by the windows of the sandwich shop, and satiated with the huge delicious vegetarian sandwiches, we did some shopping up and down Telegraph Avenue in the stores while also perusing the sidewalk vendor goods. We ended up purchasing a few cheaply priced mostly noir DVDs in a record and movie store. Then it was back across the Bay Bridge to the girls.

It was late in the day by the time we got up to the room after turning the car over again to the valet. We took the girls out to the ever-faithful St. Mary Square for a short walk. Bea was able to squeeze out a firm turd even though we thought she'd be empty after all that diarrhea earlier in the day. This confirmed that her new nickname really fit her. We laughed, thankful that she was back to normal and was able to wait until we got to the park.

On our way back to the hotel a homeless man asking for money approached us. B.B. began to snarl and bark at him for some reason known only to her. We guessed maybe she thought he was going to attack us and was being protective. She'd never acted anything but nice to other people unless they took her by surprise. She usually was friendly to strangers like she had been to the dog walker that afternoon, but took an instant dislike to this raggedly dressed, rather pungent man. Perhaps she hadn't liked the way he smelled. Whatever the reason, we scolded her for her bad behavior.

"I think B.B. doesn't like the homeless," said Kel somewhat under his breath, after he gave the

157

man his spare change which sent him on his way to panhandle elsewhere.

Since we'd eaten those giant sandwiches rather late in the afternoon there was no need to eat again. We spent the night watching TV in our comfortable room while the girls snored away in their beds and dreamed of dog parks maybe. Or B.B. might've been dreaming about what she was going to do to that car valet or the panhandlers.

The next day was sunny and warm, a rather rare phenomenon in San Francisco, where Mark Twain had said, "The coldest winter I ever saw is the summer I spent in San Francisco."

We decided to take the girls and shop in Chinatown again. Not that we wanted to buy anything, we just wanted to be out in the beautiful weather, so we took off through the green-roofed gates right across the street from the hotel.

There were workers on strike and protesting loudly when we walked by. They had picket signs with some reading, "Locked Out!" I never could tell what kind of job they were locked out of. On down the way there was another man who had a large sign with huge red and black lettering saying, "NO SEX" in red letters. That certainly got Kel's and my attention. Between those two words in smaller bold black print it said, "UNLAWFUL." Then in the "O" of "NO" it had the word "AIDS" in yet smaller print with more even tinier print below that. We didn't have the time or inclination to read all the smaller words, so we never did quite figure out exactly where he was coming from. But Kel did stop to take photos of both unusual sights. All this just added to the mystique showing that you never know what you'll see in a big city, especially San Francisco.

Lost on the girls, they were only interested in the smells they were finding all over the sidewalk, buildings and drifting on the breeze.

Since we'd been there before, we didn't spend long in Chinatown. We wandered over to the financial district which was quiet on a Saturday. One of the iconic Powell and Mason cable cars stopped to pick up some passengers before it took off and passed by us as we were making our way up one of the busy streets. Kel got a shot of it loaded with smiling tourists, some of whom seemed to be getting a kick out of our girls who were staring back at them with open-mouthed smiles. On top of one the hills Kel got a beautiful photo of the Transamerica Building, its pyramid shape topped with the pinnacle spearing the bright, clear, blue sky as the sun beamed down on it.

Before leaving for the family gathering, we gave the girls one last visit to our true-blue St. Mary Square Park. Bea didn't let Kel down, she gave him a smaller "treasure," and this time B.B. gave me one as well. We picked them both up to deposit in the treasure-chest trashcan nearby.

It was with trepidation that I crept through the front door of the hotel held open by the smiling doorman for B.B. and me since I expected the valet to be standing out there with my key in his hand. Fearing B.B. would cause a scene by barking and snarling at him, I was ready to shush her as soon as she began. I was able to nip her noisy salutation in the bud much quicker than in the past few incidents. But still, he was made quite aware that B.B. had the memory of an elephant and would never forget that he'd surprised her. The valet and B.B. exchanged intense looks

159

noiselessly as she stretched out her neck and laid her ears flat while pulling harder on her leash as she tried to get closer to him.

Arriving at my cousins' house in Oakland, we made our entrance. Jim and Rosalee were busy in the kitchen. Their daughter, Greta, her husband, John, and their two children, Eileen and Tim, were there. So was their younger daughter, Eva with her husband, Stephen, and their two children, Klehri and A.J. The grandchildren were born at the same time nearly which made for a very neat arrangement. Eileen and Klehri were eleven, and Tim and A.J. were six. Being closely bonded to each other, besides being cousins they were very close friends. Two other men were guests as well. One named Anton is Klehri's godfather and the other, Eddie, John's brother.

The wine flowed liberally as it always did when we congregated at Jim's home. The long Victorian dinner table was large enough to accommodate all fourteen of us and was laid out with a place setting and enough chairs for everyone to sit comfortably. We were all in high spirits with so much to visit about and so much wine. In mourning about the horrid election, we didn't let it cast a pall over our good time. Drinking to soothe and comfort ourselves, and being merry anyway, we bemoaned the prospect of having to put up with the "W" Administration for another four long years.

The women and Jim who is a fine cook, had outdone themselves. There was an abundance of delicious food, much of it vegetarian, which was eventually spread out across the elegant table. What a banquet we had with more wines being served along with the meal.

160

Rosalee had confided many years ago about how Jim would serve the cheaper wines early in the evening, then when he and everyone else had gotten pretty toasted, he'd break out the high-dollar wines so his guests could taste them. She always giggled about this because she felt he should've done it in reverse so his guests could enjoy the pricier wines while they were still sober enough to really appreciate them. We had to agree. But she guessed that it just took a certain amount of wine to loosen him up enough before he'd part with some of his more expensive bottles from the cellar. We laughed together fondly about his eccentricity, and we were at liberty to do that, being just as eccentric, if not more so.

Kel took a multitude of photos some posed and some candid shots, so we could capture everyone - smiling faces all around. Our girls had a fun time too since the children especially wanted to pet and play with them. Most of the adults were dog lovers so they made over them giving them lots of attention. The girls in return were on good behavior and responded lovingly to the caresses and baby talk. When we first took them into the flower-laden backyard Jim showed us where we could house them, so they'd be safe from wandering away and possibly getting into the street. His circular-shaped sunroom on the back of the house with glass windows all around was where we put our girls so they could be part of the family reunion but not bother Jim's two pet cats. The wise cats made themselves scarce during the time Bea and B.B. were there. We extended their leashes out as far as they would go, tied them to a sturdy table and placed a bowl of water in the room. Seeming quite contented with their situation they didn't even get their leashes tangled up.

Too soon it was time to say our goodbyes to our precious relatives and the new friends then let the girls leap into the Car-Car for the trip back over the Bay Bridge to a lit-up San Francisco and our snug hotel room. Another wonderful visit was behind us with lots of stimulating conversation, flavorful wines and luscious dishes shared with people we loved and didn't get to see often enough. Making the most of our short time there, we filed away many happy memories. As we drove back Kel and I talked over a lot of what had been covered that night and compared what we'd each heard from the different people there. It had been such a lot of fun! We were both a bit melancholy knowing it would probably be quite a long time before we'd get to see them all again. Leaving our family was never easy just as leaving San Francisco was always hard. I thought of the words to that song Tony Bennett made famous which my sweet mother and I loved so dearly, "I left my heart in San Francisco." It rang more truly now than ever before. A piece of my heart would forever be in the Bay Area with my first, second and third cousins.

Chapter 7   Barn Burner - Almost

By the time the four of us made our last journey over to the reliable St. Mary Square I was ready to leave the big city behind in favor of a smaller community. We both had our fill of the noise, traffic, fumes, and constant trips to let the girls do their business. After all, we ARE Okies and like the open spaces and fresh air. Big cities were enjoyable briefly, but we never wanted to stay very long. Seeing so many people trooping up and down the street after a few days made me long for the smaller towns with smaller populations and sprawling countryside. The restricted space in our room and having to summon the car every time we needed to go somewhere had worn thin. I dreaded the packing of the car puzzle because I was afraid the ardent bellhop would be on duty and raring to help us load it in a frenzy. If I didn't want to be rushed, I was certain that Kel wouldn't want to be. Hurry is hardly even a word in his vocabulary.

After the girls had their walk and were fed, Kel and I quickly dressed and put the finishing touches on our packing. As usual, I plugged in our car refrigerator so it could get cold before transferring our cold foods into it from the refrigerator in our room. After checking with Kel to make certain he was ready to start the toting and putting together of the car puzzle, I called to get the car brought to the curb.

Stealthily we snared a cart and piled it high with our belongings by hanging some off the hooks as well. Then we made our way down the elevator and to our freshly delivered car. Relieved that the bellhop was nowhere in sight, we hurriedly packed in our stuff always keeping to the proper loading order. Then we high-tailed it up the elevator again for another big bunch of stuff while looking furtively over our shoulders for a bellhop ambush. Without his help, thankfully, we were able to take our time and get it all packed. Kel went to retrieve the refrigerator while I went to the front desk to request our bicycles be brought out from the storage room. Once the Little Refrigerator That Could was safely set into the back area and plugged in, Kel went to take a last look around for any items we might've left behind and to bring the girls down before closing the door for the last time to our itty-bitty but well-decorated room. Our

163

habit of inspecting the places we stayed right before we left helped to keep us from losing things.

B.B. didn't get to say a ferocious "Goodbye" to the valet since she wasn't down there when he made his hasty exit once Kel had tipped him generously for putting up so good-naturedly with our feisty Little Sprite. Since her bad behavior embarrassed me, I was glad that she hadn't had the chance to "bless him out" doggie style as the last thing she did before boarding the car. Miss Bea, always the gentle little soul except when it came to food handouts, followed B.B. into the car as usual. Kel strapped the bicycles into the rack while the girls settled themselves comfortably in their backseat. The big load-up went much smoother than I expected.

We pulled into the La Quinta in Bakersfield in the late afternoon. Just as I'd anticipated, our room was spacious and comfortable. The girls seemed very pleased with it as they cavorted around and explored its expansiveness. Bea's jovial grin was spread wide over her cute face, and B.B. rushed around investigating every smell left by other dogs who had stayed here. There was a cart without a bellhop attached to it and no car valet to hide the car away in a secretive place making it much easier to move in at our own pace. It was more relaxing here, but I understood why the big hotels have all those employees. They need to make a living too, and most people enjoy being helped by them. I didn't really begrudge them that they were fervently doing their jobs; I just couldn't take it for very long. Kel and I as born-and-raised Okies, are more small-town than I thought.

Since it was Sunday, we wanted to watch all our good TV shows, so we put off going to eat dinner and merely snacked on some of our chips we'd brought along. After the last show ended at 10:00 we went next door to a Denny's where they're open 24/7 and we know we can always get a good veggie burger.

Unexpected entertainment was provided by a big group of teenaged girls dressed in the puffed sleeve, high-necked garb we routinely associated with rather severe religious groups. They were seated at two tables which had been pulled together to form one that would seat all of them comfortably right near where we were in a booth by the windows. Their regimented "uniforms" also included their hairdos which ranged from tight buns or ponytails to puffed up ratted hair styled in an old-fashioned 1950s era beehive. Without the enhancement of any make-up, their faces were as God had made them. During our meal we stole quick glances at them after they'd looked us up and down when we first came in. Every so often out of the corner of my eye I caught them studying us. Kel who's enormous eyes provide him with superior peripheral vision, later told me that he saw them inspecting us considerably when they thought we weren't looking. I'm sure we looked like a couple of freaks direct from the Haight to those strait-laced young ladies. But they were having such fun breaking bread together on a Sunday night possibly after a sweaty rolling-in-the-aisles, blood-pumping, speaking-in-tongues, fire and brimstone church service which really worked up an appetite. People looking as weird to them as they did to us weren't going to spoil their good time. We felt no malice towards them, just a slight curiosity about how different their lives must be when compared with the way we'd been at that age. From their familiar demeanor with the place and each other I guessed that this was most likely a regular Sunday night event. Kel and I were tickled about the fun they were having just being

165

teenagers. After all, teenagers ARE teenagers. The blissful, somewhat repressive lifestyle we assumed they must be living intrigued us. Feeling no bad vibes from them they didn't seem to be judging us either. Even though we had only driven about three hundred miles, we had come to a completely opposite end of the political and cultural spectrum - Bakersfield was about as different from San Francisco as the moon.

It was mid-morning when we finally checked out and hit the highway the next day. The sun was brilliant and warm as it climbed in the sky. I was thinking about the place we were going to stay. It sounded wonderful from what I'd read online. This is a resort of several different, assorted-styles, self-contained houses called The Forest Houses in Oak Creek, Arizona. Each of them has a descriptive name, which fits the house, and they are in the forest just a ten-minute drive away from Sedona proper. Our house is named The Barn House. I guessed it might be shaped like a barn and was excited about staying there and exploring the red rock area. Our two-night stay would allow us some time to ride our bicycles somewhere nearby. Since we'd hauled them all the way across the country we wanted to get in a few more rides before arriving home.

Darkness came early, so when we were nearing our destination, while following the directions we'd printed out, it got just a little hairy. Driving slowly along the curvy road in the mountains close to Sedona, then pulling off to head down a rather primitive, dirt road we had to cross a stream of swiftly running water in the pitch blackness of early nightfall. Kel and I were almost afraid to drive into the rushing water after seeing many reports cautioning motorists never to drive into running water. But we had to get past this flowing stream to arrive at our house in

166

this mini village. Deciding to give it a try, I crossed my fingers. The sound of the rushing water was more frightening than the limited view we had of it. I was able to ease the car through it, not too fast, but not too slowly either, and we didn't get swept away or stuck. But during the fording we were both nervous and then grateful to get out safely. I think it might've been less scary crossing in daylight.

The Barn House was sure worth the long drive, the dangerous curvy mountain road and the little bit of panic we experienced at the end. It was family-sized so for just the two of us with our girls it seemed immense. I never really figured out why they named it The Barn House because it was such a lovely place. But it was two-story and spacious kind of like a very modern, upscale barn. When we opened the unlocked door as we'd been instructed to do, we could hardly believe our good fortune. This "cabin" had all the comforts of home complete with a large kitchen featuring every appliance, even a dishwasher, in an open setting with the living and dining rooms. There was a wood -burning stove in the living room next to a comfortable, cushiony sofa and some easy chairs with a coffee table placed just perfectly in front of the sofa. The dining room had four chairs at a large table on which the key to the place was waiting as we'd been told it would be. There was one bathroom in the downstairs then a twirling spiral staircase led to the upstairs bedroom which had two skylights in the roof and beautiful views of the forested mountainside out of its two windows. Heavy wooden beams in the upper part of the ceiling hung over the king-sized bed. When I saw those, I thought maybe that was why they called it the Barn House. There was another convenient bathroom in the upstairs as well. Out front was a substantial patio made of the area's native red rocks sunken into concrete. We were in "Red Rock Country" after all. It didn't take us long to decide that this was another place we'd want to return to in the summer. This and Cayucos were our favorite new places on the trip.

As the porch light spread its wide beam enough for us to be able to see to unload the car, we felt our energy returning after the long drive since we'd been wowed by this beautiful house. Transporting all our possessions didn't seem nearly so tiring. The girls approved of the place too as evidenced by the big smiles on their faces when we let them out of the car without their leashes so they could be free to mark and sniff everything around the outside of the place. When they went in B.B. sped through the whole place sniffing upstairs and down. She had no trouble with the spiral staircase after Kel took her up once showing her how to negotiate the tiny steps. Bea kept her exploring to the lower level as she was afraid to attempt the spiral staircase. But the grin on her face showed that she was delighted too. They were even happier once they had their food.

"The girls should be fine while we're gone since they've had a good break and been fed. I'm so hungry."

"I'm hungry too so we can go any time you want," Kel replied.

Making our way out wasn't nearly as alarming as when we came in an hour earlier. I felt assured that we could cross the gushing shallow stream and survive. We carefully drove through some more mountainous terrain and then down into Sedona in about ten minutes where we scanned the main drag for a possible restaurant where vegetarians could eat.

168

Upon our return to the girls who were fast asleep in their beds which I'd carefully placed in the living room, Kel picked up some of the wood that was stacked outside on the patio and built us a warm fire in the wood-burning stove as the night had gotten quite chilly. We turned off the radio station we left playing on the computer and slid one of our new film noir DVDs titled "Sudden Fear" into the slot for viewing. There was no TV so since we had the DVDs we'd bought in Berkeley, we thought that would be good entertainment for the evening. It seemed later than it actually was because it had gotten dark so early. There were very few people staying here during this time period, so it was unbelievably quiet and dark in the woodsy area outside. We didn't even have to worry about the girls barking or disturbing anyone. The movie was exciting and suspenseful. Being such big fans of that genre, we enjoyed watching it even on the computer's small screen. The crackling sound of the fire filled the room making the air toasty for us and our dreaming girls. Life was very good out here in this wilderness.

I awoke refreshed and ready to take on hiking and biking and anything else we could figure out to do to make the most of our full day here in the stunning landscape. In the daylight when I took the girls outside of the house, I could see that there was a graveled trail which started just beyond our patio next to the creek which was flowing merrily along singing its little tune as it bubbled over the rocks. I took the girls for a mile walk down and back on the trail through the trees where the birds were beginning to awake and chirp happy to be alive in this paradise. Bea was on her usual scavenger hunt, and B.B. was eyeing the trees for squirrels who might be lurking in them. Many of the trees were evergreens like pines or cedars, but there were some

169

whose leaves had turned a bright yellow color. I could see now that our house was the last in a long line which curled around on a couple of short country lanes. We liked the isolation of it and the unique character of each individual house. I tried to imagine how it would be during the summer months when it would be crowded with lots of people and their children and dogs.

After the girls had been fed Kel and I ate some of the goodies we brought with us for a small breakfast, and then set about getting ready to ride our bicycles. Transporting them on the car we made our way over to Slide Rock Park not far away. Kel had read about it online and thought we might be able to ride in it. Our bicycles were hybrids which are blends between mountain bikes with fat tires and "road" bicycles with extremely skinny tires. We thought they'd be perfect for riding between the red boulders on the soft dirt or even on some of the smoother huge, flat rocks. The majesty of those towering red stones stunned us as we picked our way carefully through the park. The scenery demanded photographs, so we stopped many times and took pictures of each other with Oak Creek in the background and the huge bright scarlet rocks always present.

"I read online that there have been over eighty westerns filmed in this area," Kel said.

"I can sure see why. This is amazing scenery," I marveled as I glanced around in a circle on one of our picture-taking stops.

After riding for quite some time we thought we better go back and give the girls a break.

"I'd like to bring the girls back here to Slide Rock so they can sniff around and enjoy this gorgeous place," I said. Kel was for it; after all, it was their vacation too.

Soon all four of us were treading among those rocks and boulders when we came to an abandoned house that had obviously been built many years before using the red rocks native to this area. The small structure was in a decrepit condition the roof having been blown off at some earlier time but still standing. Later, Kel climbed with his girl, Bea, down the large rocks which formed a kind of treacherous stairway leading to Oak Creek way below. B.B. and I chose to stay up on top of the huge, flat rock formation. They both looked up towards us with the creek rushing behind them between the enormous pinkish slabs of rocks on either side of it, and I snapped their photo. It made this magical place more enjoyable having our girls with us to enjoy the beauty of the weather and scenery. Coming back down near the entrance to the park, we saw an apple orchard where all the leaves had turned a golden color. I'd been given a book called A Thousand Places to See Before You Die at my retirement party the previous April. After viewing all the breathtaking scenery, it was easy to understand why the Red Rock Country of Sedona was one of those places listed. That book had influenced us to come to see this distinct part of Arizona for ourselves. We felt its mystical nature.

The spell was broken when I consulted my watch and said, "We better take the girls home if we're going to have any time at all to ride our bikes in town or shop." Kel was agreeable but reluctant.

As soon as we opened the door to the Barn House, we smelled burning plastic! It didn't take long to figure out what was on fire. The kitchen had cabinets with protruding small lights at the bottom of each one, so we quickly found the source of the odor and smoke.

The day before when we unloaded, I had placed our little refrigerator out of the way for safe-keeping underneath one of those lights. I flicked the light on without thinking much about it before we left for Slide Rock Park. Once the light bulb heated up enough by being on for well over an hour it melted the plastic handle because it had been touching it. There were no open flames fortunately, and I swiftly removed the fridge from under the cabinet and turned off those lights. But the damage had been done, and we now had no handle on the top of the Little Refrigerator That Could. In its place was just a scorched, discolored, melted mess and about a quarter of what had been the handle. I was sorry about the loss, but what really caused us both the greatest concern was that I could've easily burned down the whole house with my careless behavior and lack of awareness that the protruding light bulb was touching the handle.

"Oh, my God, Kel," I shrieked, "What if we'd been gone longer? I could've burned down this beautiful place!"

" I know," he admitted, "And what if we'd left Bea and B.B. in here? I hate to think what might've happened, " I could hear the worry in his serious tone of voice.

"I promise I'll be much more thoughtful and careful in the future. I'd just die if anything bad had happened to our girls!"

" I know you didn't mean to do it, Baby," he said lovingly, "But you and I must both try to be a lot more careful from now on. We sure dodged a bullet on that one."

We were both thankful that the only thing harmed was our refrigerator making us have to rethink now about where to put it in the car so we'd be able to take it out for our picnic lunches. Never again would Kel be able to lift it out of the rear through the back window since there was no handle now. Finding another place to fit it in where it would be accessible was a minor inconvenience compared to what could've happened had we not come back and discovered my error when we did.

But since we were on vacation, we were quick to shrug it off putting it behind us so it wouldn't spoil the rest of our day. This would be our last chance until next summer to see more of this amazing area. We loaded our bicycles on the car again to head for the main drag. Scrutinizing the whole cabin for anything that might cause trouble while we were gone, since we'd decided to let the girls stay and rest while we went into town, we looked around more carefully. After checking closely, we were satisfied that everything was fine. Surely no more fires or other hazards would happen. After going through our goodbye ritual, we took off to make the short drive.

Riding our bicycles around on the streets of Sedona for about an hour was the perfect way to see a lot more of the town. The shops looked quite interesting, so we stopped at a bicycle rack and locked them up securely.

Sedona has four main energy vortexes. When I looked at a drawing in a shop illustrating their spinning pattern it reminded me of the way tornadoes in Oklahoma twist and spin in frightening and physically dangerous manners. A vortex is the funnel shape of anything spinning like a whirlwind, tornado or even just water going down the drain in your bathtub. Another place where you can easily see the spinning reflected is in Sedona's Juniper tree branches. Wherever the energy is the strongest is where the tree branches have more of an axial twist. The lines of growth have more of a sluggish spiral shape than just going straight down the branch like Juniper trees in other areas which don't have vortexes. Sometimes the branch can bend due to this helical effect.

We saw Bell Rock and Cathedral Rock from a distance. There's a vortex in the creek right next to Cathedral Rock and its energy surrounds Bell Rock. This is truly as mystical and magical a place as I'd already thought. Many people come to Sedona to seek out this energy and soak it up. We discovered that there are many New Age shops which cater to them offering items associated with mystical and spiritual guidance. No wonder Sedona is nicknamed "a spiritual Disneyland." People from all over the world come to experience the four main vortexes' energies and healing powers and to grow spiritually.

"Funny how we just happened to come here because it was a good place to stop on our way home that my book recommended," I mused after we studied the information in one of the shops.

"I'm familiar with vortexes," he answered me, "And there really IS something healing and spiritual to the energy they generate."

I am always amazed at my husband's wealth of knowledge he's amassed over his life. Kel has always devoured books, magazines and anything he can get his hands on to read, so I was not surprised that he knew about so many things that were absolutely brand new to me. I'd not read the variety of publications that he had having instead concentrated on true crime, history, or adventure books and of course, books about dogs.

The sun was nearly gone when we got back to our homey cottage and our patient girls who were waiting for their break and even more importantly, their suppers. While Kel built a fire as the night air was already getting chilly, I took the girls for a short walk around the neighborhood to see some of the other houses. A little while after Bea wolfed down her food she indicated that she needed to go out again by standing at the front door and looking back at us over her right shoulder where we sat on the couch. I let her out on the patio and turned on the porch light so she could see and so we could keep an eye on her as well. As we watched she began to eat grass as if she were starving.

"Bea's eating grass," I informed Kel who was sitting on the couch in front of the fire while I observed her.

"She must be trying to make herself throw up," he sighed.

"Well, she hasn't thrown up yet and she's eaten a whole bunch of it," I fretted.

"If she doesn't chuck it soon, we'll have to haul in the pen and tarp and keep her in it. We can't just let her roam around all over the house," Kel wearily concluded.

This worried us since we were afraid that she was trying to throw up because she wanted to clear her stomach to feel better, and we weren't sure what she might have eaten on the sly to make her feel ill given her scavenging habit. Frightened that she might have ingested something poisonous that would hurt her, we helplessly watched her consume more and more of the grass bordering the patio. Our lesser concern was that if she didn't hurl right away, she might throw-up in the house because she'd eaten enough of the lawn to make ten dogs vomit.

Therefore, he got the pen and tarp and hastily set it up in the back of the living room near the spiral staircase. We no sooner had gotten it all in place and ready for her than she was at the door asking to be let in. We put her in the enclosure at once which didn't sit very well with her as she wrinkled her face even more than usual as she studied the pen. We were thankful that we could contain her to avoid a possible messy clean-up later. This time it was B.B. who could've pranced around in front of Bea in her prison saying, "You dished it out to me in Chesterfield, sister when I had to be in that cage, but now it's my turn to show you how it feels." But instead, she just came over closer to where we were seated on the comfortable couch and lay down near our feet to enjoy the warmth of the fire.

We settled in to watch "A Clockwork Orange" on our computer. We'd seen it many times before but always enjoyed viewing it again, and I was glad we'd bought that DVD in Berkeley.

It would be a fun way to spend our time on this crisp, clear night in front of the sizzling fire. As we watched the flames, we found our eyes drifting over to where Bea had lain down resolved to her new location. We kept looking at her mouth to see if she was showing any signs of getting ill.

It had been quite a remarkable day with the fire destroying the handle of the new refrigerator on its maiden voyage and Bea's devouring what seemed like a cow's equivalent of grass. Astoundingly, she never did throw any of it up. We had to make her stay in the pen overnight, but there was nothing in it the next morning except her and the water bowl we'd furnished. We found it odd, to say the least, but were very relieved that she was fine showing no sign of eating something bad for her as the new day dawned.

Chapter 8   Santa Fe, Amarillo, and Home

"We've been gone exactly two weeks today," I announced as I served Kel his coffee in bed upstairs.

"Well, how about that," he responded, poking fun at my obsession with dates and time.

I was up for a couple of hours by the time I woke him, and the morning ritual was accomplished. We'd be driving on to Santa Fe for a one-night stay as we made our way homeward. Since it was a relatively short drive, we wouldn't have to get around quite as early as we had when we'd left Bakersfield, so I let Kel sleep in.

After we loaded nearly everything into the car, Kel placed the mangled refrigerator behind my seat on the floor. That would be its new spot so we could have easier access to it, and luckily,

177

the cord was long enough to still plug it in at the back. It was time for the usual dog race between the girls to the Car-Car with the usual results. Before we pulled away, I booked the Barn House to return to in late May which always makes leaving a place less glum.

Once we forded the rapidly moving stream for the last time and drove up the curvaceous road through the mountains Kel asked, "Could we please stop up near the summit so I can take some pictures of the valley below before we leave it behind?"

"Okay, we don't have to drive as far, so I'll find a place to pull off," I said being game as well for more photos of the lovely scenery.

Sure enough, there was a scenic turnout not too far after his polite request. We let the leashed-up girls get out with us to take one long last look at the valley with Oak Creek meandering through the evergreens and the orchard trees while the rust-colored boulders stood like monuments rising out of the dust. It was a scene of absolute serenity.

Leaving the mountains behind it was a much simpler and faster trip into Santa Fe, a new place to us. Pausing for our lunchtime routine, Bea made us laugh when she almost bit off our fingers to get at the bits of food offered her. It went totally against her otherwise gentle nature. Her food exuberance showed no discrimination between food and finger. B.B. was quite the opposite as she accepted the tidbits we held out to her, being careful to gingerly nibble, very aware of our fingers.

The Santa Fe Sage Inn was no luxury motel. Oh, it was clean enough with all the necessities, but best of all, it was saving us a little money. A pleasant surprise was the free breakfast.

178

As Kel savored his coffee in bed the next morning he blissfully said, "This is my favorite thing every morning."

However, I was experiencing a touch of homesickness and wanting to sleep in my own bed.

"Now that you've had your coffee please get some clothes on so we can go eat our continental breakfast and then get ready to go," I cajoled.

"Okay, but I just hate to cut this short - I enjoy it so much."

The drive to Amarillo was so quick that we didn't even stop for a picnic lunch. We were hoping to visit Palo Duro Canyon just outside of Amarillo, but we decided there wasn't time for it on this trip and promised to save it for another time. As we got closer to the Texas panhandle city the cows alongside the highway became more abundant. B.B. began to prick up her ears and barked at them to say, "I'm back and ready to take on any one of you!"

We noticed that she couldn't discern cows when they were packed into the immense feedlots on the outskirts of Amarillo. In other words, she couldn't see the trees for the forest. To her they must've just looked like a big mass of moving color and shapes with their heads over the long troughs as they ate the grain meant to fatten them up. Even when Kel pointed out the window at them and we both said, "Cows," she looked where he was pointing but didn't bark. She just kept looking blankly in their direction as we sped by. To a couple of vegetarians those feedlots were nightmarish, and the smell horrendously assaulted our noses even with all the windows rolled up.

Late that afternoon after losing an hour on Central Time we checked into the inexpensive

179

chain motel and got everything taken into the small room quite easily as there were no stairs to climb, and I parked the car right out in front of our door. It seemed like a trade-off. The less expensive motels with smaller rooms had at least two things going for them: they saved travelers money and were quite accessible for moving in with no hassle. But the rooms were very little and there were no free breakfasts included. The girls were happy to disembark and settle in. The motel itself was right on the main drag of this Cowtown. Once the settling in and feeding were taken care of, Kel and I left to look for a place where we could eat.

This turned out to be a marathon of hunting because we decided we wanted pizza. There was every kind of fast food joint you could name along this strip, but we didn't see one single pizza place. Astounded by this, we searched from one end of the strip to the other then went back over the ground we'd already covered thinking we must have missed a pizza place in our haste due to the plethora of signs blazing invitingly in the dark sky. But there were no pizza establishments that we could see. We just about gave up, and I was turning the car around dejected that we'd have to settle for something that we didn't really want to eat, when Kel spotted a bright, neon sign flashing "PIZZA" out of the corner of his eye way in the distance out past the edge of town. At that moment, I thought it was the most beautiful sign I ever saw. I put the pedal down hard as if my foot were connected to my growling stomach, and we made it there in record time. Going overboard, we had a feast eating way too much of the dish we so craved.

The next morning when I weighed on the scales that I always insisted on bringing with me, I was a pound heavier due to the indulgence. But I didn't mind knowing I could work on losing it when I got back home and started exercising more. That was one thing about traveling in the car, there wasn't much chance to get a good workout just sitting. What's more, I wasn't about to work out in one of the exercise rooms offered by some of the places we stayed. I'd rather gain weight than do that. It is the same way at home. My stationary bicycle gathers dust in the basement as I always want to either ride my bicycle or walk out of doors. Spending time out in nature is always most important to me. Whether I am exercising or not, I never can stand to be cooped up for long.

I was up earlier than usual in anticipation of seeing how our place had fared while we were gone for over two weeks. All the regular morning routine went smoothly. Kel and I just ate some granola bars that we brought along with us as our breakfast since I was anxious to get on the road home and didn't want to take extra time to linger over a breakfast at a diner.

"Why don't we just put on our clothes and pack up to go without bothering to clean up?" I ran this by Kel. "We could get home early that way. Besides, we have our bowling league tonight."

"If that's what you want, we can do it," he gave in knowing how much I wanted to get back to our beautiful place and admitting, "It does make sense to get home early for our Friday night bowling league." We knew Jeff and his girlfriend were expecting us to be there.

"We can clean up in our own bathrooms when we get home," I said pointing out the obvious.

We were on the road at an unbelievable time for us especially with all the belongings we had loaded. The weather was clear, and we made good time. As always, Bea took it good-naturedly when B.B. sometimes stepped all over her while berating the numerous bovines.

181

Our woodsy neighborhood was a very welcome sight as we pulled through the towers at the front and wended our way across the first bridge by the big lake, up the curving slope to the fork in the road, then taking a left there and heading west across another bridge until we turned onto our beloved street. Everything looked normal as I steered the car up the driveway. I was relieved to see that nothing was amiss. There in the little tree was B.B.'s old, skunky collar hanging just where we left it after our first dog vacation.

As we entered the neighborhood, I rolled the windows down completely to see if the girls could figure out where they were. When they smelled the familiar scent of their turf, their eyes lit up and they both stood in the backseat with their pointed ears pricked up even higher. It was unmistakable that they, indeed, realized they were back to their home sweet home. The closer we got the faster their tails wagged as the familiar smells of the neighborhood filled their noses, and they both grinned with wide open mouths.

Opening the car door, we let them bound out without their leashes since they were safe in their own front yard. They immediately took to sniffing and marking as if it were their jobs. It was evident they were as joyful as we to be back. Kel and I were working on the huge unloading when the housekeeper showed up. It was lucky we arrived back home when we did as she didn't have a key.

"How was your trip?" she queried, as we all walked into the house together with the girls dancing all around her feet begging for attention.

"It was fantastic! I'll tell you all about it," I said as I smiled broadly and closed the front door behind us.

TRIP 3   Don't Mess with Texas!

Chapter 1   A Tale of Three Cities

As quickly as B.B. could change directions on the beach while chasing a flock of seagulls, and even faster than Bea gulping down forbidden food, the holidays sprang upon us. We welcomed the new year of 2005 at the end of the whirlwind of activities which began with Thanksgiving and proceeded through my 52nd birthday and on through Christmas. Staying home during all of this we only went to Tulsa to do a little shopping for gifts at one of their big malls. But in early January the wanderlust began to sprout in my heart and soul. The traveling seed had been sown again by looking at the photos of our first two dog vacations in the special scrapbooks. B.B.'s collar still smelled like skunk juice where it hung on the little tree branch across the driveway. A constant reminder of that first dog vacation we could see the humor in our past predicament and laugh about it now. Kel and I spent many an evening in the new year cuddled up with the girls by the fireplace reminiscing about those first two dog vacations to the east and west coasts which stoked the embers of desire to pack up Bea and B.B. and travel once more.

"I think I'm ready to take another trip somewhere," I said one bright, mild January day when the sun glistened warming the trees outside our huge living room windows.

"Me too. Where would you like to go?"

"Somewhere without a lot of snow or ice, but that's close by, and where there's a beach," I answered right away.

When Kel and I put our heads together a plan began to take root to travel to several cities in our neighboring state, Texas, as they didn't usually have very much snow. We could drive short hops to spend a little time in each place as we made our way down to Padre Island, a popular destination with college kids for Spring Break. Visions of the beach with warm, sunny days where B.B. could chase seagulls and Bea could sniff the sand for tidbits of food flowered in my head. Kel and I agreed that it would be the perfect place to go, so we booked dog-friendly places to stay in Fort Worth, Austin, and San Antonio with a longer stay in Corpus Christi. Making our way back, we would stay in Austin again and Euless, a suburb of Dallas, where our good friend,

185

Paul was living, and maybe get to see him while there.

Embracing optimism, we'd take our bicycles along to ride whenever and wherever the chance presented itself. So, we put the rack back on my CRV.

I should've known this trip would not bloom into as much fun as the other two had been because a bad omen warned us as we were preparing to leave.

That departure morning dawned fine with the glorious sun shining considering it was late January. I was anxious to get on the road and trying to hurry Kel along while becoming more and more perturbed. It seemed like the more upset I got the slower he became almost as if he was doing it on purpose.

Having already taken about half of our belongings out to the car I wanted him to help with the other half.

"C'mon, Kel! Hurry up and let's get this stuff packed in now," I shouted in a loud whine from the doorway leading to the garage. "What the hell are you doing? I want to get on the road!"

He knew from past experiences that I was working myself up into a frenzy which would only spiral out of control with more delay. In response, he rushed across the living room faster than normal.

There was a sudden loud crash, and I ran back in from the garage to see what had happened. My poor man was lying prone on the brick steps that lead to our sunken living room near the big, round, red chair large enough to hold two people. He'd hit his head on the bricks as he tried to

186

run out to squelch the fit I was throwing. He was lying there trying to recover.

"Oh, my God! What happened?" I screamed, already guessing the answer which wasn't pretty.

In a weak voice he answered, "I was attempting to keep you from going crazier and hit my foot against the red chair and my head on the bricks when I broke my fall."

" I'm so sorry, Kel. Are you hurt? I shouldn't have been in such a hurry," I felt as deflated as a wilted daisy while the tears welled up in my eyes.

 " I think I'm okay, but I just need to lie here a minute to get my breath and pull myself together. I got my bell rung just now."

I looked at the left side of his head once he was able to get up and stagger slowly to the half bath nearby for a look in the mirror. He had scratches there from the brick floor and some on his left hand where it had taken the brunt of the fall. The only consolation was that none of them were very deep. But, nevertheless, I felt terribly ashamed and guilty because my caterwauling had been the cause of his accident.

"I'm so sorry, Kel! Do you think you'll be okay to travel?" I asked sadly as more tears fell down my cheeks.

"Yeah, I think I'll be okay. Just give me a few minutes to rest then we can go ahead and get the remaining things in the car."

The girls, sensing that something awful had happened hovered around him as he lay on the red chair for a few more minutes. But once he recovered, he got up and said, "I guess I'll be

187

okay, so let's get the rest of these bags packed and get going."

I wasn't going to dwell on remorse. Learning a valuable lesson that day I determined that impatience only caused more accidents resulting in more delays. Bea and B.B. were way ahead of me in that respect because they always showed such patience with us. Dogs can teach us many of life's lessons if we're just willing to learn from them. I wished I was more like them before I'd been so impatient with the dearest person in my life. Kel was as forgiving as any dog would be.

He was feeling chipper by the time we reached the motel in Fort Worth. There was a little path in a green space just made for dogs to relieve themselves - perfect for our short hikes. La Quintas could be counted on to be very comfortable and hassle-free about dogs.

Making our way back to the girls after supper we lay on the king bed to watch some TV before turning in. I hoped Kel wouldn't be sore the next day from his tumble on the hard bricks, and I wished for a better day tomorrow for us all with no more mishaps. My silent pledge was that no matter how long Kel took I would not yell at him again about hurrying up. He was patient with me most of the time.

The day dawned cloudy and cool for our trip on down to Austin, the capital of Texas. It is like an island in the middle of the state because their politics are more liberal and the culture is diverse with an immense music scene featuring all styles. There are many art galleries and the whole atmosphere is quite cosmopolitan.

The University of Texas is located there as well, made infamous by a twenty-five-year-old student named Charles Whitman who shot people randomly out of the top of the bell tower on the campus in 1966. He'd already murdered his mother and wife before he began his rampage from his perch where he killed fourteen more people and wounded thirty-two others using a variety of guns including rifles, a shotgun and handguns. Having been a former U.S. Marine he was an engineering student when he snapped and massacred all those innocent people. The police were unable to apprehend him for over ninety minutes until he was finally shot and killed by Houston McCoy, an Austin police officer. Kel was in high school, and I in junior high, but we remembered it well. At that time, mass shootings were not as plentiful as they, sadly, are nowadays. The world was shocked by what had happened. And we're still shocked these days, but it's not quite the same since we experience them way too often now.

It rained on us the entire trip. I decided that people in Texas are just crazy when it comes to driving on the rain-soaked roads. They drive too damn fast for the conditions. We saw several wrecks along the way that were probably caused by hydroplaning due to driving at breakneck speeds. As I always like to make good time, I had to slow myself down and be extra careful about controlling my speed. But having experienced hydroplaning once, I became a believer about slowing down during rainy weather.

My "accident" happened when Kel, Jeff, who was just about ten years old at the time, and I were driving back from Kel's parents' home in Tulsa. I was driving my 1974 Pontiac Grand Am and the rain had just begun. We were going west out of Tulsa and nearing the smaller town of Sand Springs. Driving my usual speed of seventy mph, I suddenly could feel the car sliding and

189

out of control as I tried to steer. The car was turning sideways on its own.

"We're out of control!" I screamed as my eyes, which must've been as big as Frisbees, turned to meet Kel's, which immediately filled with concern and dread as he took in what I said.

This was a divided highway with two lanes on each side and my car was careening right towards the center median area which was just a large grassy ditch. Jeff was in the backseat sleeping since it was dark and late at night. Jeff could always sleep in the car even with rock music on the radio blaring in his ears.

Kel, seeing the headlights of the cars coming at us in the other two lanes across the divide, braced himself with his hands against the dashboard for the impact he believed was inevitably coming. It all happened so fast, yet it felt like a slow-motion dream as it played out.

Later Kel told me that his brain flashed in the split seconds between my dire announcement and the resolution of the accident with the realization "Here, I've hitchhiked all over America and been in some desperate situations with some of the rides I got, but now I'm about to die in a stupid car crash with my precious son and the woman I love who wouldn't slow down on the rain-slick roads. Of all the irony!"

My only thought, as I fought the wheel for dominance, was, "Oh, God, I've killed us all! I'm so sorry!" The approaching headlights were coming nearer and nearer as my burnt-sienna-brown car blended with the dark night sky and turned as the passenger's side slid towards the oncoming traffic. The cars weren't slowing down - we were invisible to them at that angle. We slid off the side of the road into the deep grassy median ditch, heading straight for the other side of the

190

busy highway. The car threw up a wave of water as it plowed sideways through the culvert median with the headlights of the approaching cars shining like lanterns through it from the other side. It was all very frightening. But, miraculously, the car sank into the soft muddy earth and came to a stop in the middle of the divided area. We had escaped the worst. Of course, I desired to get back on the road as soon as possible once I realized that we had all survived. Being in shock and feeling as if I'd just awakened from a disturbing nightmare, I put the car in reverse to back out. Itfelt like I could deny what had just taken place and wipe it all away if I could just get out of the ditch.

"Whoa, whoa," said Kel, "Not so fast. I don't think you're going to be able to just back the car out of this deep ditch filled with water."

He was right; we weren't going anywhere. Not one minute passed before a pickup truck pulled onto the shoulder right ahead of us and two young men jumped out.

"Do you need us to pull you out?" one of them asked.

"Well, yeah, if you can." I was quick to take these saviors up on their offer.

They hooked their tow rope up to the front of my car like a speedy pit crew during the Daytona 500 and with their powerful truck, slowly dragged us out of the deep, muddy grass.

"Thanks so much," I said as I handed them a $20 bill for their trouble.

"They must be driving around all over this area looking for people to pull out of ditches," Kel reasoned.

"Yeah, I bet you're right. They'll make quite a lot of money on a night like this."

191

I drove slower all the way home the rest of that rainy night. And from that time on whenever it rains on the highway, I slow down not wanting a repeat of what had happened those many years ago. The outcome might not be as good the next time.

The Lost Parrot Cabins outside of Austin are dog friendly, and in a woodsy location. We were safely there by late afternoon. It was a very gaily colored cabin in bright pinks, reds, green, and yellows as the name would imply with a large, handy deck off the back that faced a dense forested area. It was covered, so it was the perfect place to store our bicycles which gave us more room in the cozy cabin. The place had a full kitchen, king-sized, comfortable bed and a spacious living room with a TV. It was quiet and peaceful out there in the country especially as we were the only guests. We'd gotten used to that since our first dog vacation when we'd stayed at the Morning Glory Inn in Pittsburgh and then with Sonny, our landlord, and just one other guest over in Knoxville at his Maplehurst Inn. Traveling out of season made for very few tourists.

Kel has an old friend by the name of Frank who lives in Austin, so he gave him a call, hoping that he might meet us somewhere to eat supper. But since he is a busy attorney, we didn't get to see him. Besides we hadn't given him any notice that we were coming.

After a wonderful vegetarian feast at the West Lynn Cafe in Austin, we drove back to where the girls slept in the comfort of the dry cabin while the lulling rain was still coming down. It was pleasant listening to it hitting the roof while watching TV in the wonderful king-sized bed.

The rain had stopped by the time I woke up the next morning. I could hear roosters crowing as I sat out on the deck to drink my coffee and write in my journal. We really WERE out in the country. The air cleaned by the rain felt cool and smelled fresh. I'd already taken the girls out for a spin and fed them before I sat down on the deck furniture to record my thoughts. It was very pleasant sitting out there and reflecting on our trip so far as I always did when I wrote. But after I finished writing my usual page, it was time to make coffee and serve it to Kel in bed. I enjoyed pampering him on the road, and he was always appreciative.

The day was kind to us as we didn't encounter any more rain. We had an easy, short trip and arrived by midafternoon to the La Quinta in San Antonio. We were there so early, and it was such gorgeous weather that we took the girls for a long walk down the famous Riverwalk along the San Antonio River. Our little ladies were on their best behavior as they strolled along with us, Kel guiding Bea while I restrained B.B., who wanted to chase the pigeons. Paying no attention to B.B., they were busily snatching up scraps of food scattered on the sidewalk before Bea could get it. She didn't give a whit about the pigeons - she was only excited about the food.

Several people we passed complimented the girls on how nicely they were acting or how cute they were. Of course, I was asked by one lady what breed they were, and I gave my standard answer of Shep Peis which always made me smile. She seemed to accept that as a real breed as she smiled back, nodded and went merrily on her way.

Our friends and bowling partners, Cory and Matt, had recommended the margaritas at a restaurant by the name of Rio, Rio. Happening upon it, we stopped to try them out. The girls were able to sit down by our umbrella table which was right next to the river as it flowed silently by. There was a little wrought iron fence that separated the courtyard area out in front of the restaurant from the steep bank of the river, and they made themselves at home next to it under the table legs near our feet while we enjoyed our margaritas. Matt was right, they were quite tasty. As we were sitting there basking in the sunlight and sipping our drinks, a flotilla of ducks came paddling by. B.B.'s ears pricked up even higher and her tail curled tighter as she spotted them. Jumping up as if to chase them, I held on to the leash to keep her in check. All she could do was bark until they disappeared out of sight down the meandering path of the wide waterway. Once we finished our drinks it was time to walk back to the motel and feed the girls. They were ready for their food and then a nap.

Kel and I journeyed back over to the Riverwalk later in search of dinner. We left the girls resting with the TV on. After scrumptious meals, we made our way over to The Alamo which we'd seen before on another trip. Lit up now that night had fallen, it was interesting to see it again and contemplate the history that had transpired on this spot. Davy Crockett and Jim Bowie, who had fought and been killed here were the famous defenders most associated with the horrible battle. I couldn't help but think about the war cry which Sam Houston had used to rally his troops six weeks later: "Remember the Alamo!" As I stood there in solemn silence and ruminated on all the brave souls lost there, I felt a spooky sadness creep into my heart.

The girls were sleeping soundly punctuated by Bea's loud snoring, normal for her when she was in a deep sleep. Their trek along the Riverwalk had really worn them out. Kel and I were tired too, so we didn't spend a lot of time watching TV. Since tomorrow was a Saturday, we

194

wanted to be well-rested, so we could look around at their market in full swing. After shopping a bit, we would take off for Corpus Christi and Padre Island for some fun in the sun on the beach.

Chapter 2 Rainy Daze

Before setting off for Corpus Christi, we had time to tour with the girls around our area in San Antonio. Mercifully the sun had decided to shine on us making our excursion pleasant. While shopping at their flea market, we didn't find anything that we couldn't live without. Then we stumbled upon the home of the famous writer, O.Henry. Posing on the small front porch with Bea and B.B., Kel snapped our photo. The house was marked with a sign reading, "O. HENRY HOUSE   VISIT FREE." It was an extremely tiny, plain, modest house made of some kind of stones that were held together by concrete which had all been painted white. The trim around the little front window was a reddish-brown color as was the door which had a window on the upper half. There were three brown wooden posts in the front bracing the small roof. The porch was only about twelve feet across with similarly colored brown boards as flooring. It was quite unobtrusive, certainly not what I'd expect a famous short story writer's home to look like. The front window had the curtains drawn tightly which made it impossible to see in. There were some more windows on the side, but it was the same story at them, and the house was locked up tight.

Having nothing more to see except a very tall tower, we hurried back to pack and leave for points south. The sun was still shining as we said goodbye to San Antonio. My mind filled with visions of Bea and B.B. on the beach we were traveling to today crowding out any other thoughts

195

as we took to the highway.

Our arrival in Corpus Christi at another La Quinta was again in midafternoon as it had been a fairly short, uneventful drive. The clouds came back and were still with us when I checked us in. Once we unpacked all our belongings in the proper order and got everything up into our good-sized room, we headed straight to the beach. Since I'd expected it to be like Cayucos with lots of sunshine making the water glisten as B.B.'s feet flew across the sand chasing the seagulls, I was sorely disappointed when we parked at the deserted beach where the wind was blowing like a hurricane.

We let the girls out with just their choke chains on. There was no need for their leashes due to us being nearly the only creatures on the beach. Even with the wind's force, there were still bedraggled seagulls searching for food. B.B. spotted them right away, and her merry chase began, making us laugh in spite of the weather. But our laughter was short-lived. The cold and damp with the unrelenting wind pounding on us the entire time was hard to take. This Mistral wind combined with the dampness energized Bea who began to caper about much more than she had in Cayucos. That surprised all of us yet not as much as what happened next.

B.B. turned and sprinted as fast as she could over to where Bea had paused for a moment to catch her breath. When she got up close to Bea she didn't stop running. Instead, she broadsided Bea like a charging bull, knocking her down roughly onto the sand. It was like a linebacker hit, and it upset Bea terribly as evidenced by the shocked, frightened look on her face. B.B. took off at a gallop back along the beach once again chasing the seagulls as both of us yelled at her,

196

scolding her for knocking her sister onto her side. Rushing over to a stunned Bea who was still trying to come to grips with what her younger sister had just done, we tried to comfort her over the howling wind. Still admonishing B.B., the ever-present nuisance carried our voices away. Giving no thought to the open field tackle, our little Black Seal merrily raced farther down the beach nearly outrunning the gale blowing behind her.

Our attention had been focused so heavily on our older dog's amazing exuberance that we were not sure if B.B. had been trying to play with Bea to make the most of her burst of vitality, or if she had been maliciously exhibiting jealousy.

We cautiously helped Miss Bea try to stand up. Comforting her as we both spoke softly and stroked her beautiful, soft, beige fur, we observed her movements. When she tried to take a step, her right back leg wouldn't work, and we were horrified that she was holding it up so as not put to any weight on it.

"Oh my God, Kel, her right back leg is injured!" I wailed while the wind nearly drowned out my voice.

" I can only hope she hasn't broken her hip," Kel fretted into the unceasing din.

"I'm scared to death that she might have," I plaintively spoke, aware of how old and fragile Bea was.

"Well, I for one, am ready to get them both into the car and get out of here. This trip to the beach has lasted long enough," Kel announced.

Knowing he was absolutely right, I too felt just awful about our poor Sweetness. So, Kel

197

whistled for B.B. who obediently came dashing to us her eyes all lit up from the fun she'd had scampering after the seagulls. Kel picked Bea up in his arms and carried her gently to the car while I spoke those two magic words, "Car-Car," to B.B. She made a mad charge to be the first one into the backseat. We let her jump in before Kel tenderly placed Bea beside her. It was a melancholy drive back to the motel, as we were both out of our minds with worry and wondered if we should try to find a veterinarian who would be open late on a Saturday.

We were a solemn group on the elevator. Bea was still holding her foot up, and B.B. must've sensed that something was amiss because of our lack of conversation all the way to our room. Her ears were splayed, and she didn't make a peep the whole time either. Kel carried Bea into our room while I held B.B. on her leash so she wouldn't run through the door first. Once inside, Kel suggested, "Why don't we give Bea an aspirin for the pain. It'll help and might make her drowsy so she can rest a little after her supper." Luckily, I'd brought aspirin in the little first aid kit I always carried in my cosmetics bag. She swallowed it thinking it was a treat, for even in pain, Bea could still eat. I fed them both their food since I didn't want Bea's empty stomach to become upset by the aspirin.

"I see the collision hasn't diminished her appetite," I said, feeling hopeful that she'd be just fine. She ate every bite of her food while standing on three legs and was even feisty enough to bark at B.B. while guarding hers as usual. It seemed that she might be returning to her normal self. When she finished licking her empty bowl, she limped over and lay down in her bed to sleep. We turned on the TV for some news but watched her instead. B.B., exhausted from her run on the beach, settled down in her bed for some needed rest.

About an hour later Bea stood up, and we noticed that she was putting weight on all four feet as she walked over to get a drink from their water bowl. My heart sang with joy at the sight!

We were thankful and relieved to see our little sweetie moving about with no apparent pain. That aspirin must've helped. Neither of us had been very hungry after that incident, and once my fear had been reduced, I began to feel my empty stomach protesting.

"I think we should go eat now," Kel suggested.

"Yes, now that Bea seems to be feeling better, we can find a place for supper."

A Thai restaurant fit the bill. We had a luscious meal there then proceeded on to a movie theater to see a film called "Sideways." It was the perfect comedy to take our minds off our sorrowful day at the beach. We verged on hysterical at some points because it was quite funny. A large amount of the movie made us laugh hard like we hadn't laughed in quite a long time. Paul Giamatti, Thomas Haden Church, Virginia Madsen, and Sandra Oh were the main stars. The film was about two middle-aged men who were kind of losers going on an excursion for a fun-filled week to concentrate on tasting wines all around Paso Robles, California. It was sort of their last hurrah before one of them got married. Being old enough to have experienced more of life, we really enjoyed the picture. Kel, in his video critic role, felt it wouldn't be nearly as funny to younger people as it was to people our age who could relate to it better. We took pleasure losing ourselves in it for a couple of hours.

We were smiling and still discussing it when we opened the door and saw our precious girls sleeping. Bea's loud snoring assured us that she was fine and getting some healing sleep. B.B. awoke instantly when we entered the room. I gave them their last break, at which time Bea walked without any problems.

"Bea's almost got her prance back," I happily related when we came back in. "I think she'll be good as new by tomorrow with some more rest."

The next morning the wind had died down a little, but the clouds were still hanging around making everything look like a black and white movie. When I took the girls out for their morning walk Bea's prance had fully returned. We always loved to see her special kind of walk with her tail held up straight and her gait as if she were walking on her toes putting one foot directly in front of the other like a supermodel on the runway. We always called it her "prance," and I was so grateful that she'd recovered it. Still wondering what had gotten into B.B., I had to put any anger at her behind me and go on as that question would never be answered. Bea barked at B.B. over the food again and stood on all fours to eat every bite licking her bowl at the end. B.B. ignored Bea's barking as usual, and once I'd put the doggie appetizer on hers, she polished it off.

Kel, after checking the weather said, "If we're going to ride our bicycles, we'd better do it this morning."

"Yeah, since we've hauled them all the way down here, we need to ride them at least once."

A little breezy, the wind wasn't nearly as strong as it had been yesterday. Plus, even though it was cloudy, it wasn't raining or even drizzling. Not sure if the weather would hold, we were willing to take a chance.

Scoping out the heavy traffic, we opted not to ride out on the main roads. Afraid of being hit, it just looked too suicidal since everyone was driving at least ten miles over the already high speed limit. With no lights on our bicycles and the murkiness of the day, we feared drivers might not see us until it was too late. Caution was the way to go, so we just rode around in the back neighborhoods close to the motel. But at least we got to ride for a little while. Before we made it back, the wind began to pick up and blow like those famous Santa Ana winds in California, so we called a halt to cycling farther out and circled back.

It was time to get bathed and dressed then look for something, preferably indoors, to fill our time. Our plan of the fun-on-the-beach vacation days was withering on the vine. There was no comparison even remotely to Cayucos.

"I came down here once over Spring Break when I was in college, and it was just like this - all cloudy, cold, windy, and rainy," Kel explained. "I never came back here ever again until now."

"Well, I'd never been down here before, but I don't think I'll ever want to come back again. In fact, I never went anywhere except Bartlesville for Spring Break. I always went home to see my parents."

Kel smirked at my reply, saying, "I took an adventure during that time, and you think going to see your parents was better?"

"Well, I thought it was the right thing to do instead of just running off."

Kel looked up a mall on the computer that was close to our motel, so we went to look around there.

During our visit we over-indulged at the buffet in a restaurant called Souper!Salad! With many good vegetarian choices, it was too enticing for us not to eat there. After stuffing myself on far too much of their tasty food, I remembered why I always tried to avoid buffets.

Upon our return to the motel, being overly optimistic, we decided to give the beach another try. B.B. once again chased the seagulls as they were still around even though it was cold and cloudy. Bea plodded along slowly with no limping, her nose to the sand hunting for bits of food. However, the disagreeable weather drove us from the beach after a very short time.

Needing to warm up, we opened a bottle of red wine that we'd brought along. It always warmed us up, and drinking some might raise our spirits a little too since the somber weather had dampened them considerably.

"The wine has whetted my appetite," I announced. "I think we should go pick up a pizza from that place down the street and bring it back here to eat in the room with the girls. Then they can have some of the crust like they usually do at home."

He was fine with that, as he wanted to watch our favorite TV shows on a Sunday night. The pizza was surprisingly delicious, and the girls' upraised tails reminded us of shark fins swimming around the edges of the bed as they begged for and enjoyed the small bites of crust we shared with them.

After a spate of TV viewing, it was time to give the girls their last break before tucking

202

them into their beds with my little poem I always whispered to them. The sleepy day had made us want to sack out as well, so I said a silent prayer for a dryer day tomorrow as I heard the rain begin to pitter-patter on the roof.

When I stepped on the scales the next morning my depression deepened due to the weight I'd gained on this woebegone, wet trip. Why was I surprised after all the food we ate the day before? Plus, we'd piled on more calories by splitting a bottle of wine, not really a low-calorie drink. Still, I tried to keep up my spirits and not give in to the gloomy mood that was threatening to overtake me. The rain was falling as I took the girls out for their obligatory walk. They did their business rapidly wanting to get out of the rain.

Thankfully, this would be our last day and night here. I resolved to do something fun even with the rain pelting down and to cut back on my eating to lose some of the weight I'd gained over one day's wild abandon.

"What do you think we ought to do today for fun?" I asked as Kel sipped his coffee in bed while the girls slept.

"Is it raining?" he queried.

"Can't you hear it? I think it may rain all day!" I moaned, as I pondered if Kel was going deaf.

"Well, I guess maybe we could go to another movie if you want. Obviously, we can't ride our bikes or take the girls out to the beach again."

"You're right about that. We'll have to look on the computer to see what's playing. Maybe there will be something we want to see," I said hopefully.

To clear us all out of our room so the housekeeper could clean it, we took the girls and drove over to the visitor center on Padre Island. It was the motel's policy for safety's sake of not allowing their housekeepers to clean unless the dogs were crated or out of the room. Not wanting to crate them in their pen with the tarp, we preferred to take them with us. The room needed a good cleaning, and Bea and B.B. were pleased to be going anywhere. The weather was still miserable, so we didn't waste any time going out on the beach after we'd looked around in their visitor center while the girls stayed in the car with the wind howling around them.

I wondered, "What was I thinking when I imagined it would be warm and sunny like a tropical island?"

When we arrived back to the motel our room was freshly cleaned. Once the goodbye ritual was done for the girls, we set off to a matinee of "The Aviator" starring one of our favorite actors, Leonardo di Caprio as Howard Hughes, the quirky man who'd had quite an interesting life. When I got a whiff of the popcorn, my good intentions about dieting fell apart. It was comfort food, and comforting was what I needed right then. We forgot about the rain and cold wind for about two blissful hours. Even though it was pouring down as we left the theater, as if it had saved a cloudburst for our exit, I still felt better after being immersed in such a good film.

Our returns to our girls were always sweet when we saw their happy, expectant smiles with their little ears raised up and tails wagging to say, "We're so glad to see you. What are we going to do now?" They reacted as if they hadn't seen us in ten years never failing to lift my

204

heart out of the doldrums just by being their unconditionally loving uncomplicated selves. Every time I walked in my eyes would turn downward scanning the room for their upturned faces like parents look for their small children.

Later, Kel and I went to a nearby T.G.I. Friday's because we knew they had good veggie burgers. More comfort food would satisfy us for our last supper in Corpus Christi.

Spotting a Petsmart right close to the restaurant I suggested, "Let's go get the girls and bring them back to the Petsmart so they can sniff around and have fun looking at all of the treats and dog toys."

"If that's what you want, my Baby Duck, that's what we'll do." Kel had nicknamed me Baby Duck way back when we first knew each other. He gave me this pet name because when my temper flared once, he said, "You're about as ferocious as a baby duck." I dubbed him Woolly Bear as a term of endearment due to his beautiful long naturally curly locks and his tall stature.

Going to a pet supply store was a fallback position since it was an inside activity we could all enjoy. The girls had a fine time perusing the aisles and pausing to sniff at some of the more tempting foods and treats. Eliciting laughs from us, they scampered around from bags of food to the hogs' ears along with other animal parts for chewing on which were awfully disgusting to us. Their noses led them to an array of dog treats in packages and toys of all shapes, colors, size, and textures that squeaked or made realistic animal sounds. Bea mostly concentrated on the food and treats while B.B. stuck her nose into everything within reach. At one point, Bea started to help herself to one of the unwrapped dried pig ears that was on a low shelf which she could easily reach. She was just going to steal it as Kel pulled her away quickly. If he hadn't noticed, we had no doubts that she would've snuck it right out of the store. We cackled over her stealthy antics and ended up buying them a box of "healthy" treats which we opened once we were all back in the room. They were thrilled with their delicious dog "candy," and begged for more, but I had to ration the treats since Bea already looked like she was about to pop.

The relentless rain was in the background, as we could hear it beating down on the motel's roof when we settled in for some TV that last night. Happy that we'd be leaving this place tomorrow, I said a fervent prayer for the rain to end during our trip the next day.

The little children's song I'd taught my kindergarteners every year floated through my head, "Rain, rain, go away. Come again another day."

Before going to bed, I did some packing to get ahead on the loading. My heart was again hopeful before I sank into sleep longing for the sun and wanting a favorable outcome when I stepped on the scales the next morning.

Chapter 3   Monsoon Lesson

When I awoke the next morning, the incessant rain was beating on the roof sounding more like a funeral drum to me. The girls had to get at least a pee break before I fed them, so we ventured out just enough for them to accomplish this, then hurried back in out of the chilly drizzle. My feelings matched the gloomy atmosphere with the only bright spot being that we were leaving today. What a sad surprise it had been to come down here and find that the weather

206

wasn't any better than in Stillwater or maybe even worse. Determined not to come in January ever again, I still had to admit that it was nice to get away for a short while despite the uncooperative weather. When I stepped on the scales, I'd surprisingly lost a half pound, so I felt a little less dejected already.

Alternatively misting then pouring on us, we carefully motored back to Austin at a slower speed than I normally would drive. The girls slept a lot since the dark cloudiness was very conducive to that when combined with the car's motion. Not bothering to get out for a picnic, we just snacked on some junk food out of the fruit basket as we drove along. Seeing how delighted Bea and B.B. were to be traveling again even in the crummy weather, I resolved to model after them and make the most of this trip, although there was not much to see, and the rain was always tagging along with us.

Upon our arrival back at the Lost Parrot Cabins we were given the same snug cabin we'd stayed in on the way down.

The landlord questioned me as he checked us in, "Why did you decide to come down here in this season?" He'd probably been wondering that ever since we'd checked in the first time.

"I was under the mistaken impression that it would be warm and sunny down here and on Padre Island. I thought we'd be getting away from the cold weather in Stillwater."

"I'm sorry that it's been raining on you so much. But this is our monsoon season," he apologized.

"Oh, that's okay. We still had a pretty good time even with the bad weather," I responded not wanting to make him feel guilty over things he couldn't control.

"Was it bad down in Corpus?" he asked.

"Yeah, the wind was blowing like crazy when we went out on the beach, and it rained most of the time and was cold," I answered truthfully. "But we saw some great movies and ate lots of good food, so we had some fun there anyway. When the rain let off, we got to ride our bicycles once for a short time."

"Well, I hope ya'll won't hold it against us and come back sometime to stay here in a better season," he invited as he smiled and handed me the key.

"Maybe some other time," I fibbed, while thinking secretly to myself, "I'm not ever planning to come down here again." But I didn't say that out loud to him, of course, as there might be a chance about as probable as me running for a political office that at some remote time in the future during another season we might try our luck here again. Even in my present dour frame of mind, I wasn't willing to rule that out.

We moved into our cozy, warm cabin rapidly as the rain pelted us steadily.

"Let's go to the West Lynn Cafe again for supper," I suggested. Just thinking of that totally vegetarian gourmet restaurant made my mouth water. It wasn't often that we went back to a restaurant on the same trip, but this place was extremely special to us.

"Sounds perfect to me," Kel agreed.

The food was superb just as we'd known it would be. Less crowded on a Tuesday than it had been on the Thursday when we'd eaten there before, we were able to get a first-rate table right in front of the twenty-foot high windows facing the street. People were still braving the rain to scurry along on the sidewalk with their umbrellas and ponchos or raincoats shielding them.

Satiated by the amazing food, we drove back to the girls for a session of TV before turning in. They'd already been sleeping in their beds while the TV hummed monotonously in the background accompanied by the ceaseless raindrops on the roof. As soon as we came through the door they awoke, and we greeted them with the customary petting and sweet words said in that gentle tone of voice which they understood more than the words themselves. The ever-present rain was still tap dancing on the roof when we all settled in for a good night's sleep.

Early the next morning, I took the girls out for a quick break then went back to bed. As I lay there, I began thinking more than usual about my wonderful parents and how much I miss them and how life used to be. My thoughts turned to how fast time has flown by. I took a silent accounting of how all of a sudden, I'm fifty-two, retired after a twenty-nine-year career of teaching, my parents are gone, and I'm lying here wondering where the time went. Vowing that morning to try harder to follow Bea and B.B.'s blissful example of enjoying every day to the fullest from now on, even during the stressful times, even on rainy or snowy days, and even when it seems like everything is working against you. I also resolved to be nicer to Kel and treat him better by not taking him for granted and showing more patience. Contemplating my life so far must've been brought on because we were making our way back home.

The girls were standing by their bowls, ready to be fed which snapped me out of my reverie as well as out of the comfortable bed to serve their dog food. Then I made coffee for myself as I grabbed my journal and pen to begin writing in it for the day. The sun was out and with its glow came the promise of a pleasant day to travel. No rain! Once I finished putting some of my bed-bound reflections and resolutions in my journal for posterity to serve as reminders, I took the girls out for a leisurely walk looking in wonder at the sky to see if there were any threatening clouds. Tonight's destination was Euless, Texas, a suburb of Dallas, where our good friend, Paul, lived. When we got unpacked in our room, we'd call him, hoping to meet him somewhere for dinner.

What a difference the sun made as it beamed its golden light on us while we drove up the highway towards Dallas. Cheering us all, B.B. barked at the many cows and "horsiecows" out in the fields. Bea barked right along with her clueless as usual as to what she was barking at. The sun's embrace, along with the uproarious barking lightened our hearts making us laugh. Kel and I talked of our home, our parents and other relatives, Jeff, our old friends and memories of days gone by. Recounting some of the same stories which we'd shared before about the past, we found them to be funny and some, poignant.

"It's funny how we always start to reminisce about home and the past when we're driving back, don't you think?" Kel observed.

"Yeah, I guess it's because we're thinking about settling back into our regular lives. I don't really understand the phenomenon, but it happens every time we're on the road home," I agreed.

The pleasant weather buoyed our spirits and changed my mind about the trip being a waste.

210

Now I could clearly see that it really hadn't been that bad. But I still felt that we'd not want to drive down there during their monsoon season again. Ignorant that Texas even HAD a monsoon season, this little dog vacation had taught us that lesson.ir

When I checked us into the La Quinta in Euless, I was surprised to find out that I was their "Guest of the Day" which entitled me to a nice package of goodies. That put the cherry on top of the delightful day we'd had. Once we got all our belongings moved into the large room, we

tried to reach Paul. Kel had to leave a message on his voice mail as he didn't answer. We surmised he must be working and couldn't answer his phone.

Paul did professional photography of church congregations for publication in the yearbooks they put out annually. Parishioners could purchase those to keep a record of their friends and acquaintances who were fellow church members. I have a photo of my parents that was taken at their First United Methodist Church for the yearbook. Since they are gone, I treasure that picture of them together smiling in their Sunday best more now than when they first gave it to me. Paul probably was not the one who took it, but he had made me familiar with the process. He was very good at his job and shared many an entertaining, funny story about his experiences at the various churches where he worked. Sorry that we couldn't reach him, we were hungry for supper, so we quickly found a Thai restaurant nearby.

Paul called long after we'd gotten back while we were watching TV. He was quite disappointed that he'd not reached us sooner as were we. Just as we'd thought, he'd been working late that Wednesday night and didn't check his phone until quite a lot later. That church was having a service, as so many do on Wednesdays, therefore, they requested that Paul come after the hour-long church service ended and get as many pictures as he could. It was too late for him to come over to our motel because I was getting very sleepy. We promised Paul that he could come and see us in Stillwater whenever he had some time off from his job.

The drive up the interstate the next day was fast, easy and rain-free. Luckily, there were no close mishaps or traffic tie-ups to delay us. B.B. barked her little heart out as there was an abundance of cows and "horsiecows" grazing in the fields or eating hay their owners had provided for them in feeders. The brilliant sunshine improved our mood tremendously.

Rolling the windows down once we crossed through the gates at the entrance to our lovely neighborhood we wanted to see if the girls would recognize any of the smells and know that we

212

were home. Again, as on our return from the west coast, they became very animated as their ears stood up higher and they wagged their tails the closer we got to our driveway. Everything looked normal in our beautiful, woodsy subdivision. We were relieved to see that our house was still standing undisturbed. Not that we really thought it would be in tatters, but because we live somewhat secluded with all our trees surrounding the property masking the house from the street, we never knew what we might find upon arriving. The houses were built on expansive lots of no less than two and a half acres so we weren't within close proximity of our neighbors and couldn't look over to see what they were having for dinner like in some of the fine, newer, more expensive neighborhoods where, ironically, the houses are built nearly on top of each other on extremely small lots. Kel and I found it odd that people would pay a huge amount of money for a beautiful home built so close to their neighbors. They were willing to forfeit a little of their privacy by living there. It seemed weird to us but being tolerant people, we just shrugged it off.

"The girls were so good on this trip," I said as we began the large unloading process. I observed them as they sniffed around all over the area bordering the driveway checking out the trees for squirrels and the scents of the other dogs and abundant wildlife who must've come by.

"Yes, they were perfect little ladies again."

I was in a hurry to move everything into the house and just dump most of it in the front entry way with the promise to put it away later when we had more time. Since I'd stopped the delivery of the mail and newspapers before we left, there was a pile of them greeting us. Those would have to be gone through tomorrow as there was no time to look at them now. Our main objective

213

was to get cleaned up and take care of the girls so we could go to post bowl in our league. This trip hadn't been as fun as the first two dog vacations, but it hadn't been a total washout either since we'd all had some good times despite the ugly weather. I was glad to be home safely again and to have learned a lesson: don't mess with Texas in January.

Our post bowling went well - we won three out of four games. The personnel meeting we had to attend as Humane Society of Stillwater Board members turned out to be nothing to worry about and was actually quite good. Everyone there felt the same way about the director as we did - disappointed in his performance. One of the Board members who might've dissented was Absent which was another pleasant surprise. So, in all I felt like things had worked out better than we'd thought. The last best thing was that while we'd been away no dogs were destroyed due to lack of space on the city Animal Welfare side of the shelter. The Humane Society of Stillwater, a no-kill shelter, had been able to absorb all of those whose time had run out. Elated to hear that reported at the meeting made it a happier homecoming.

Trip 4   Return to Sedona

Chapter 1 The Tree House

I checked my calendar and discovered to my dismay that we'd have to film a wedding on the very day I'd planned for us to begin our trip to stay in The Barn House outside of Sedona. I had booked it before we left there back in November. Since I hadn't brought my appointment calendar with me, I didn't recall that we had to work. So, I called our landlady there and requested that she change our dates. Unfortunately, the Barn House had been rented for the new dates, and she only had one other house available. It was named The Tree House. Our home in the subdivision is nicknamed The Tree House due to the many large trees surrounding it so I considered this a good omen and snapped it right up.

Once we returned from our rather miserable trip to Texas the remainder of our short winter was pleasant. There wasn't much snow, and the weather was nice enough for us to take lots of bicycle rides throughout February including on Valentine's Day. With the weather so unseasonably warm and beautiful after our bike ride that day we got out my daddy's red-hot cinnamon cherry drop car, a 1965 Buick Wildcat convertible I'd inherited and took the girls for a Valentine's Day spin with the top down. They always loved their rides in that car with no head where they didn't even have to stick their noses out the windows to smell what the breeze brought them. The evening was capped off with an especially delicious dinner, a gift exchange, and romance. I couldn't have asked for a more perfect Valentine's Day. In fact, there were many gloriously sunny days all through the shortest month.

Near the end of February Kel had an idea for a party in April. We met a couple of very talented Irish musicians on our trip to Ireland in 2004. Upon hearing them play on the third day at Puck Fair we knew they were something special. Hank played the guitar and sang, and Ray played the mandolin like a lead guitar sometimes or chorded or picked depending on what the song demanded. They sounded more like four people than just two. After purchasing their CD, we listened to it over and over, enjoying it more with each playing, and I learned to sing some of the background vocals as well as some of the leads by singing along with it.

Liking what we heard, one day Kel said, "I'd like to fly them over to play a party in April here

216

in Stillwater. We could invite a whole bunch of our friends and have a blast at the same place where we had your retirement party. What d'ya think?"

"I'm on board. What a fantastic idea. But do you think they'll come?" I was a bit dubious.

"We'll have to send them an email at the address on the CD and inquire. They can only say 'no,' but they might say, 'yes.' "

That's exactly what we did and then negotiated by phone with Ray once we heard back in an email from Hank. Long story short, we booked the dates for them to come and sent e-tickets for their roundtrip flights. Our excitement about their visit was building more every day and we were quick to send out emails to our friends to apprise them of the party so they could save the date of April 22nd. We dubbed it the Irish Pub Party.

Most of March was lovely with cool temperatures, strong winds, and a few non-severe thunderstorms reminding us of spring showers to come that might turn tornadic. We spent a lot of time planning the party as well as planning a September trip to England, Wales, and Scotland which obviously wasn't going to be a dog vacation.

Finally, the day came to pick up Hank and Ray at the Tulsa airport. Thrilled, we recognized them as they came down the hallway where we were waiting. They seemed to remember us from when we hooted, hollered, and sang along on nearly every song they played that rainy August day at Puck Fair in Killorglin. Since they played mostly American music I was familiar with, and I had learned some of the songs on their CD, they asked me to sing back-up vocals on some of them. What an honor and such fun. On the two days before their performance we

217

rehearsed out on our deck surrounded by April's lush green trees and bushes. A local bar was having Open Mic Night on the Thursday night before our party on Friday and seeing it advertised on their marquee, they asked if we could sign them up to play. Taking the small stage at 10:30 finally they blew the crowd away. And again, I was invited to come up during some of their performance to sing with them. The acts that were to follow just left the building refusing to play after their stellar performance. So, they just kept going for a very appreciative crowd. During the short breaks people were coming over to ask questions, keeping Hank very busy answering them. Ray is quite friendly to people he knows but less gregarious than Hank who never meets a stranger. The party that next night was a huge success with over 150 people in attendance. Our Irish performers were a gigantic hit and it looked to us like everyone had a terrific time listening and dancing to their music. Once again, I was called up on stage several times to sing with them. Hank and Ray's visit to Stillwater was way too short - only four nights. But we crammed more fun and music into those than we'd had the whole month previous to their arrival. The weather was so warm that we took them touring around Stillwater in the red convertible to show them the sights on their first afternoon with us. By the time we drove them back to the Tulsa International Airport taking Route 66 per their request we were fast friends. Hating to say goodbye and send them off we promised to meet them if they were playing somewhere over here, and we hoped to see them sometime again in Ireland.

Now May had stolen silently in on tiptoe to blossom with red roses near Kel's birthday and our trip with the girls to Sedona. The long-awaited day had finally dawned. Knowing what it would be like where we were going made me tingle with more than the usual excitement. Of course, we weren't staying in The Barn House, but I figured The Tree House would be just as nice even though the landlady had told me it was smaller. Our weather had been unseasonably hot the day before we left with temperatures in the upper 90s. I was hoping it would be cooler where we were going.

It was a glistening, sunshiny day that was starting to heat up early and I was anxious to get on the road before the temperature rose too much as I hated to load the car and get all sweaty after being freshly bathed. Our first stop for the night would be in the old reliable town of Tucumcari where we stayed on our trip to California. It wasn't too far to drive and had several dog-friendly motels. And we looked forward to eating at Del's Mexican Restaurant again since we'd really enjoyed our vegetarian meals there previously.

It was only mid-morning but blazing with heat and humidity when we pulled out of our driveway. I didn't really care much that I'd gotten very sweaty loading the car, however Kel was terribly bothered to see me dripping with perspiration. I think he was afraid I might have a heatstroke. Now that they were such veteran travelers the girls understood the two magic words "Car-Car," and were happy to run and leap into their backseat.

We'd stopped before in Oklahoma for lunch at a rest area with tables shaded by teepees. I wanted to stop there again and was pleased that the teepees kept us fairly cool.

Gaining an hour when we crossed into New Mexico we arrived by late afternoon at the same Motel 6 where we stayed in November. The old, familiar highway made our trip quick and easy and we were glad to be back to the less humid desert air. It was even cooler than in Stillwater. The mountain rising to the south of town greeted us as we neared the exit.

Desiring to eat at Del's we were disappointed because it was closed on Sundays. So, we opted to eat at Dean's, another Mexican Restaurant.

I wondered aloud, "Do all the Mexican restaurants' names here start with D?"

Dean's was almost the twin of Del's with good and inexpensive food. Like Del's they didn't serve alcohol at that time. We enjoyed eating there too but decided we liked Del's a little better because of the atmosphere and all the scenic pictures on the walls.

After coming back to the motel and checking on our little sleeping sweeties, Kel and I rode our bicycles up and down the streets just as we'd done when we'd been there before. Our ride wasn't difficult due to the lack of hills to climb for which we were thankful after consuming so much good but heavy Mexican food.

When we rode back to the girls it was time for a bit of TV before bed. I was looking forward to staying for the next four nights in The Tree House as sleep came stealing over me.

The day dawned with gorgeous, golden light illuminating the desert. The morning routine with the girls went well. Kel appreciated having his coffee served to him in bed now that we were on another dog vacation. I hardly ever served it to him in bed at home, so he usually had to get up and make it for himself. The only days I would pamper him at home were when the housekeeper had already arrived; he didn't want to go down to the kitchen in his bathrobe while she was cleaning. After brewing the coffee I'd bring it upstairs to him in our master bedroom.

Kel looked forward to Friday each week when she came to clean. Being a night owl, he'd sleep late and the housekeeper nearly always arrived before I even woke him up.

We remembered the America's KIX on Route 66 Mainstreet Coffee Shop & Eatery just down from where we were staying so we decided to return. When we entered the place, we noticed the KIX on Route 66 place mats and asked if we could have a couple of them. We wanted one for ourselves and one for our Irish musician friend, Hank who'd been quite enthralled by Route 66 on his visit to Oklahoma. He and Ray had performed the song of the same name many times as they played places far and wide all over the European continent, Ireland, and the U.S.A. But they'd never been on the Mother Road until we chauffeured them back to Tulsa on it for their flight home. It had been their first and only visit to Oklahoma, so we wanted to mail him a Route 66 placemat as another keepsake. Knowing Hank as well as we did, we were sure he'd appreciate it. The lady who seated us was more than happy to let us have two to take with us.

We made it to the Forest Houses Resort by that evening. The days were longer than when we'd been there before, so the sun was still up as we drove across the stream where this time with the water low, we forded it easily. The place sure looked different than when we'd visited back in the late fall as the trees were in early bloom with the grass greening up.

The Tree House was up high as expected with a big balcony deck that towered above the path below and stretched across the entire width of the house. It was supported by four large wooden beams with lattice work in between them on each side. Underneath it in the open space below was where they stored all their firewood to use in the fireplace during cold weather. We could sit out there and look down on all the people coming and going. The girls loved doing this sometimes barking at the people and other dogs. And there was a good crowd with lots of children and their dogs who would bark back. Kel let our girls bark a little but then shut it down before it became too annoying. There was a wooden deck on the front as well with a large sliding glass door as the only entrance to the cottage. It was opposite the balcony and level with the ground out front built split-level style on a small hillside cliff. Shaped like an A-frame this wooden cottage had one enormous room that housed a bed and couch with chairs, a small chest of drawers, a little kitchen table, and a small but full kitchen tucked away on one side. There was a separate bathroom with a tub and shower off to the other side of the big room. The place was smaller than The Barn House, but it proved adequate for our needs. The only thing that had me even slightly worried was that there was no air-conditioning. I hoped the days wouldn't get too warm for the girls while they were staying in there when we were away riding our bicycles or sight-seeing. Upon looking around in the house more I discovered a large fan that we could use along with my smaller fan I always traveled with. Generating a cross breeze through the place would keep the girls cool. Secretly I wished that we were staying in The Barn House, but I had to get over that and not let it spoil our good time in this beautiful, mystical Red Rock Country. It was thrilling to be back.

"I'm so hungry," I whined as I glanced at my watch later in the evening. "Could we go eat at that place called The Orchards Bar & Grill where we ate last November?"

Kel, having experienced my hunger pangs many times answered cheerfully, "If that's what you'd like, my love then that's where we'll go."

I could get very "hangry" when I got too hungry for too long. It hadn't taken him long to learn not to let that happen. I guess it was due to my upbringing when my dependable mother always had our meals on the table at a certain time each day. I am a lot like her in that respect wanting to be consistent and on time keeping to punctual routines in our daily lives. Kel is more flexible and not concerned with time but humors me quite often.

We ate portobello mushroom burgers with fries and margaritas. What a wonderful vegetarian feast it was, and the drinks were superb too. Quite full and satisfied we drove back to the girls who were sweetly sleeping in their beds as the night air was cooling down the silent desert. There was no TV, so we read our interesting books for a while then sat out on the balcony talking and watching as the moon made its appearance and the stars began winking at us in the clear, night sky. Sensing the peacefulness out there the girls joined us to star gaze and breathe in the clean, cool air. Having that balcony sort of made up for not getting to stay in the larger Barn House. As we said goodnight and called it a day, we were all in a fine mood. I was counting on having some fun adventures tomorrow.

Chapter 2   Riding in the Red Rocks

Since the house had no air-conditioning, I considered it fortunate when the day dawned cool and cloudy. Kel and I would be able to ride our bicycles and not worry about the girls getting too hot. Looking longingly at The Barn House when the girls and I walked by on the handy trail right down the way from our Tree House, I couldn't help but still wish that we were staying in it.

But when the three of us sat out on the balcony while I drank my coffee and wrote in my journal my enjoyment of that made me quit yearning for something I couldn't have. As there wasn't much foot traffic below us the girls stayed quiet. Kel was still asleep until I awakened him with his coffee while the girls did their wake-up dance around the bed.

Starting our day off we took a longer walk down by the creek bubbling merrily along below us where we could see it off the cliff. The rocks sticking up like majestic monuments in the distance all around us blazed a beautiful shade of red as the sun lit them up. The cool fresh air and the caroling of the birds, who were awake now and singing their joy added to our pleasure. Once we got far enough away from the houses, we let the girls loose from their leashes but kept their choke chains around their necks to restrain them if necessary. Every so often we encountered a squirrel who would quickly run up a tree to avoid B.B.'s jaws. Her eyes lit up each time she raced over to the trunk trying to capture a pesky varmint who had scaled it in nothing flat and was chattering at her from the safety of a branch way up high. Bea sniffed for food scraps all along the way but finding none, eventually just gave up and pranced along content to just relish the beauty of the day.

We made our way down to the creek while they were still leash-free and when we got close to it B.B. jumped right in. What a surprise that was as we didn't think she'd ever do that. She swam around splashing and dog paddling like she was a Lab. Then, what I deemed a miracle happened - Bea waded in and swam a little bit, too. We couldn't believe that our pristine Miss Bea would get her perfectly coiffed fur wet. Their unexpected behavior caused us to laugh uncontrollably. Just when we thought we knew them inside and out they'd do something completely out of character, entertaining us. After their dip in the creek we set off back down the graveled trail to our cottage. They weren't young dogs, so we figured they'd want to sleep awhile after their swimming and hiking.

We knew our girls well. They both got a large drink of water at the same time crowding each other at their water bowl like pigs at a trough then lay down in their dog beds for a snooze. That was the signal for Kel and me to put our bicycles on the rack so we could transport them over to the Bell Rock Pathway for a ride. He'd deemed that our hybrids could handle it after reading about it in a brochure.

Once we began riding through the red rocks on the soft dirt, we found that what the brochure claimed was an "easy" ride was a lot more challenging for us. The sun had come out and there wasn't a cloud in the sky by now, so the air was heating up rapidly.

"Thank God you brought Gatorade with us," I exclaimed as we stopped to get a drink.

"It's always good to have something with electrolytes since it's starting to get hot now. I have Dasani also if you'd like some."

"I'm so glad that you were a Boy Scout and learned to always be prepared," I said teasing him but not really joking. Kel's ability to handle nearly any situation correctly always amazed me.

"That was one of the most important things I learned from scouting."

The rocks that were hidden from view under the soft dirt and the small crevices that we had to guide our wheels between as we wove our way through the large red boulders made the riding

slower and more difficult. But our hybrids handled it well and we were quite careful taking it

slowly so as not to fall and injure ourselves or our bikes. The scenery was breathtaking just as

we'd remembered from our short stay in November even though it had changed with the coming

of spring. Where the distant trees had been yellow, now they were green, and some had flowers

blooming. It was incredibly lovely to ride out among the red rocks with some towering above us

like a wall on both sides of the pathway. Eventually, we had to travel back to our car and load

up the red-dust-covered bicycles to drive back to the girls. After two hours with the sun beating

down on us, we became hot and tired. Most of the ride had been fun though.

We appreciated the much closer look we'd gotten of Bell Rock the pathway's namesake. It

was one of the places near a vortex and I felt the energy emanating from it but maybe it was just

because I'd read about it and the power of suggestion caused me to feel something.

When we opened the door to our cabin the girls were sleeping soundly with Bea snoring as

usual. They awoke immediately once they heard us enter the room.

"Let's all go to the Dairy Queen down the road," Kel suggested.

He didn't have to ask me twice - I was ready for a cool, sweet treat, and the girls were always

ready to go in the Car-Car. Quick as ice cream could melt in the desert sun, we put their leashes

on them and let them race out and jump into the backseat. Kel put the bicycles out on our high

balcony for safe storage. Surely no one would be able to climb onto the balcony and steal them.

After cooling off with our sweet treats we drove over to a flea market to look around for a little while. Since it was all set up on tables outside the girls got to tag along with us to sniff around. There was really nothing there that we wanted to buy but it was fun just to browse and let Bea and B.B. bask in the admiration of the shoppers. A woman asked the usual question about their breed to which I gave my standard answer. Bea lingered and her eyes grew wider as she salivated due to the variety of enticing aromas of the foods being sold. Kel had to drag her away on her leash or I think she might've stood there all day imploring a kind soul to give her a tidbit of one of their appetizing purchases. We had to chuckle over her ability to look so sad and forlorn when she wanted something. But judging by her plump body anyone could see that the dog wasn't starving.

Our next stop was a delicatessen down the road a bit farther where we bought a few necessary items for lunches like cheeses and chips. When we arrived back at The Tree House Kel used some of our newly acquired cheeses to put with our analog lunch"meat" for sandwiches then we had a picnic on our balcony while the girls sat with us and scanned the people and dogs who were walking by. There was quite a lot of barking "conversation" until Kel called a halt to it all. When "Daddy" said, "Stop!" they both settled down as they put their heads on their front paws satisfied just to observe in silence.

"Now that the day has gotten hotter, I'd like to go swimming in the creek," I sprang this idea on Kel knowing that he wasn't ever really very interested in swimming. That may have stemmed from when he swam on the team back in high school. He probably got burned out after so much practicing and competing.

"I guess we could take the girls and let them swim with you. I don't want to swim but I'll go along and supervise to make sure nothing bad happens," he said, giving into my whim.

Fearing he might change his mind I didn't hesitate to put on my bathing suit,

We were able to walk right down the trail from our cabin and scale down the cliff to Oak Creek where the water felt cool and refreshing. There were round stones to walk on in the shallow creek which was surrounded by larger gray boulders on both sides and tall, bright, green plants amidst the boulders along the edges of the water. B.B. was lightning quick to seat herself in the shallow water right in the middle of them where we could barely see her little head sticking out above the tops of the bushes.

I jokingly said, "There's B.B. in the bulrushes," and we laughed heartily at the spot where she chose to sit. The expression on her face was extremely serious considering the fun we were all having. Cackling with laughter again Kel snapped some photos of her in that position. Bea was much more reticent than she'd been earlier this morning. She wrinkled her face with concern when "Mama" waded right into the water. Standing on the large rock slab on the bank beside the flowing water she gaped at me while I sat down on the rounded rocks out in the middle. Finally deciding that it must be safe if Mama was in it, she daintily stepped off her perch and into the water where it flowed just halfway up on her legs. Kel took some pictures of the two of us cooling off in the clear stream. No matter where we were or what we were doing our girls always amused us. Their personalities were so different yet each in her own way could make us

228

burst out laughing at her antics. Quite often they did the opposite of each other. Knowing them as well as we did, we thought we could bank on what they would do in a given situation and most of the time we were correct. The surprises were what tickled us and made us laugh the hardest. I loved being caught off guard by some unknown facet of doggy thought which they acted upon. It certainly kept life lively and interesting having them with us at home and on trips. On these dog vacations, our love for Bea and B.B. grew even deeper than I ever believed was possible given how much we already adored them. It had to be due to the close proximity during our time on the road. My heart was full that sunny day with all four of us together having such a splendid time.

Tuckered out again from their hike and being in the water the girls lay down to rest while Kel and I got ready to go into Sedona to shop around and eat dinner.

After wandering in and out of the shops we went to eat supper at Thai Spices Natural. It was delicious vegetarian food. But now we were quite ready to call it a day and get back to Bea and B.B. and our inviting balcony where we could sit and relax in the cool night air with the stars and moon lying in the clasp of the dark sky. Kel told stories, and we talked late into the still, quiet night. The girls napped at our feet only stirring if they heard unknown sounds in the distance. We felt safe and contented sitting out there above the roofs of the Forest Houses below us. Being here together and experiencing this remarkable place in a different season I thought back on our very full day and my heart swelled with gratitude.

The next morning my thoughts turned to Stillwater because it was the last day of school for the children in the Stillwater Public Schools. The teachers, however, would have one more official workday before they could lock up their classrooms for the summer. Out of habit I kept up with their school-year calendar. This first year of my retirement I took a slightly naughty pleasure in writing in my journal about the time of year it was and how relieved I was to be free from all the routine school activities after my twenty-nine terms. Not having those responsibilities anymore was just fine with me. Truthfully, I didn't miss teaching whatsoever.

The sun was sailing in the cloudless sky when the girls and I sallied forth for our walk down the trail. The air was fresh and clean with a rather cool breeze. Once again, the birds were warbling making us feel as happy to be alive as they were. Our routine was the same as every other day and I loved it probably because of the old schoolteacher in me plus the fact that my mother and daddy had always maintained such a regular schedule. It had been ingrained in me from birth.

Kel was having trouble finding a good place for us to ride as we wanted to explore more of Sedona on our bicycles again. We finally opted for just a couple of short rides that weren't really very interesting or challenging. The way I perceived it was that at least we were riding and burning calories. I enjoyed riding much more than hiking due to my bad right hip. Bicycling didn't irritate my hip and make it hurt nearly as much as hiking or the worst, climbing up and down stairs. But there was some pain caused even by the pedaling.

A little disappointed that we hadn't ridden very far I shrugged it off as we transported our bicycles on the car back to our cottage where the girls were sleeping. It was lunchtime by then so, we sat out on our balcony for another picnic with some more of the healthy foods we'd purchased the day before. There was something very pleasing about sitting up high on that balcony and watching everyone meandering by. Just to relax there filled my soul with contentment. Sitting and relaxing was rare for me - I always had to be doing something. Kel was so much better at taking it easy. I always said, I'm a racehorse and he's a turtle. I never meant that in a bad way - it simply was my way to describe our personalities. They say, "Opposites attract." We are certainly opposites in that way so maybe that's one of the reasons among many why we've stayed together so long.

Once we accepted that we weren't going to ride any more for the day we decided to take the girls out for a scenic tour in the car. Kel had found something in another brochure about a drive we could make to view some of the most beautiful countryside around Sedona.

Following the directions from the pamphlet we came to what they called a "primitive road." It was that all right with lots of big bumps and dips, but my car took it well. The scenery was worth the jostling we all received while enjoying our ride. Kel took some beautiful photos of the lovely wilderness where the red rocks stood up above us in all kinds of statuesque formations while smaller rocks cascaded down the hillsides among the mostly pine trees that dotted the landscape. Each formation had layers of color, a geologist's dream. Wind and rain had worn places in the giant rocks so that some looked like they had faces. In others where we discerned shapes of animals or people, it led our imaginations down many paths. Purple thistle flowers were in bloom, splashing their color throughout the area. Huge slabs of red rock resembling a

231

stage descended on several different levels each jutting out from the one above it.

"I'd like to go eat now, Kel."

"What sounds good?"

"I don't know. Why don't we just go look around in Sedona and see what they have to offer for vegetarians."

"Okay, that's good by me." He was easily persuaded.

Leaving the girls to sleep again at the Tree House, we took off and driving down one of the main streets saw an interesting pizza place called Picazzo's.

When we got back to our sleeping beauties our adventurous day had sparked the flame of romance in us. The girls were so much easier to have in the cottages or motel rooms than children would've been during all our intimate interludes. On our very first dog vacation to the Northeast Kingdom I had promised Bea and B.B. that if they wouldn't tell what they witnessed I wouldn't either.

Afterward we went out on our balcony to say goodnight to the calm, starry sky. We retired early in order to be rested and meet our tour guide early the next morning for our Pink Jeep Tour which we'd booked previously. So excited I was afraid I wouldn't be able to sleep but the wine and satiation kicked in and it wasn't long before I was out.

Chapter 3   Pink Jeeps, Jerome, and Invisible Mountain Lions

We all got up early not wanting to be left behind for our Pink Jeep Tour. I did all the normal morning activities involving the girls and my own coffee, cereal, and journaling. The only thing we had to forego that morning was Kel's lingering over his coffee in bed. Quick to clean up we got the girls ready to stay in the cottage for the few hours we'd be gone. Then we were off as fast as jack rabbits in the desert after our goodbye ritual.

When we arrived the person in charge of assigning us to our guide looked perplexed when she couldn't find our names on the list of those who'd signed up to go. Having already charged the two tickets on my credit card this worried us, and we couldn't imagine why we weren't registered for the 9:00 o'clock tour. It turned out that we were a whole hour early. Unbeknownst to us Sedona hadn't gone on Daylight Saving Time like other areas in Arizona. Therefore, the time was really an hour earlier than we thought. Making the most of our extra half hour we walked to a nearby coffee shop and had a cup while Kel also ate a sweet pastry for breakfast. Time seemed to drag by but finally we walked back to board the actual jeep, which was truly a bright pink, then took off for the most remote zones of Red Rock Country.

The enhanced Jeeps take tourists to places that are inaccessible in a regular vehicle. Even four-wheel-drive Hummers couldn't go into these wilderness areas. Our guide told a story about a Hummer trying to make it through this wild territory that had gotten stuck between one of the narrow passages of giant rocks and had to be towed out. We strapped in with the other four people and our guide using big shoulder and lap straps making me a little apprehensive about

233

how jerky and rough this roller coaster ride might be. There were also metal bars welded into the sides behind our seats to keep us all safe inside the vehicle. The three bench seats that held two people each were situated along the outer edges where we faced into the open middle. To shield us from the sun already high in the sky and beating down intensely was a good metal roof over our heads.

Our guide was movie star pretty in a rugged sort of way. She had long raven black hair that was pulled back in a tight ponytail and was wearing blue jeans with a long-sleeved turquoise shirt and big sunglasses. I must've looked very prissy to her in my pink shorts and top with matching pink flip-flops crowned on their tops by fluffy pink miniature pom pons which matched the color of my shorts and top exactly. I felt that the Pink Jeep Tour called for me to wear that very color having brought along that outfit. My big sunglasses were similar to hers.

The brochure had not exaggerated, and we marveled as the lovely young lady expertly guided the pink chariot out over the huge flat slabs of red rock into the most isolated but beautiful regions way out beyond the town. The going was rough and bumpy with lots of steep uphill and downhill climbing, jostling us as we laughed nervously, grateful right away for the security of the strong straps and metal bars behind our seats. It seemed like we were nearly about to tip over onto one side at times. Then at other places the front would dip so low that I'd swear we were going to hurtle end-over-end down a steep ridge. The dry heat of the desert was already making its presence known and I was very thankful that I had worn shorts. But dry heat is much better than Oklahoma's hot and steamy humidity.

234

She stopped at various points allowing us to get out of the vehicle for photos of the phenomenal landscapes. The red rock outcroppings fanned out in layers like huge steps leading down to the scrub brush on the floor of the desert below. There were large hoodoos that resembled figures standing majestically as if supervising the tourists who were snapping photos of their stark beauty. Sometimes the way the sun hit them made them a bright golden color as it enhanced their red tint.

I never doubted that a normal car or even a four-wheel-drive vehicle wouldn't be able to make it to these far-off-the-beaten-path slick rock places. Our guide explained that these Jeeps were modified and specially equipped to enable them to get in and out of these far-flung spots. Kel and I were very pleased that we took this tour otherwise we'd have missed some of the most amazing scenery the area has to offer.

Near the end we stopped in an especially stunning spot overlooking a wide valley that spread out below with the red rocks far away in the distance standing like sentries who were guarding this mystical place - the Grand Finale. The guide had us pose with our backs to the camera while she snapped a photo of us gazing out towards the rocks over the valley with our arms locked tightly around each other's waist.

She pointed out, "Sometimes it makes a better photo to have people looking towards the scenery with their backs turned instead of smiling at the camera. After all, that's what you've done most of the time while we've been out on this tour."

It made sense to us, and once I saw the photo, I knew she was right. Kel filed that bit of knowledge away for future photos with scenery in the background.

The tour had revealed about three hours of breathtaking views giving us our money's worth. Once we returned in that mechanical flamingo to our cars in Sedona, we left to check on the girls and eat some of our Thai food leftovers for lunch. Bea and B.B. were sleeping when we slid open the door. They immediately woke up clamoring for our attention which we readily gave. Then we all sat out on the balcony to eat sharing little bits of noodles with them. But the food was almost too spicy to let them have very much - we didn't want to upset their stomachs. Bea's iron stomach probably could've handled it but not B.B.'s gimpy one. And, of course, we couldn't give just one dog a treat without treating the other.

Kel had read about Wilson Canyon in a brochure he picked up somewhere along the way, so we loaded the girls into the Car-Car to take them on a fun trip to hike with us. The day was quite hot by now, so I filled their bottles for drinks while hiking, and filled our bicycle water bottles for us too. Kel packed his camera for those amazing photos he expected to take. The hike was thrilling as the girls picked up new smells in the small but pretty canyon. After looking it over we took our sweet girls back so they could nap the rest of the afternoon.

"There's a small town named Jerome over to the west of Sedona. I've just been reading about it in this brochure and it looks kind of interesting. Maybe we should drive over there and explore it a little bit," Kel proposed.

"Fine with me now that the girls have had a good break. They should be just fine to stay here and rest for a while. But I think we might need to set up these fans since it's fairly hot. I

236

wouldn't want them to get too warm in here while we're away especially during the hottest part of the day."

Kel set up the large fan at the sliding back door that led to the balcony and then put the smaller fan in the front window to draw a substantial cross breeze through the house. After he was satisfied that the fans were safe and stable to keep the girls cool, he turned music on the computer right before we left.

"You stay here and take care of this house, Bea and B.B. We'll be back soon," I said following the normal goodbye routine. They seemed reassured by the words they were accustomed to hearing as they settled down on the cool tile floor for a siesta.

The drive over to Jerome wasn't far as we traveled across an expansive valley and then up to the town built on a hillside. Reaching the main part, we were shocked at how much it reminded us of Eureka Springs, Arkansas, a little village we'd visited nine times during the 1980s and 1990s. Stepping onto the streets we had the same feeling as the first time we'd set foot in Eureka Springs that long-ago August. Our last trip there had been in 2003 before I retired when we took Bea and B.B. along with us.

Jerome had the same attributes as Eureka Springs - they were both built in levels on hillsides and had many hippie-esque shops lining the quaint streets along with freaky-looking people close to our age wandering around. We fit right in. A variety of artsy, new age stores and galleries just like in Eureka Springs lined the streets as well. We even saw some younger hippie types milling about enjoying the pleasant weather. A large hotel called The Jerome Grand Hotel had a haunted mysterious air about it very much like The Crescent Hotel in Eureka Springs that some claim IS haunted. All Jerome's crooked little alleyways even resembled those we were so familiar with in the little Arkansas burg.

Kel and I had often talked of writing a werewolf novel featuring Eureka Springs as the setting due to the narrow winding streets with spooky dimly lit alleyways, the charming but slightly eerie Victorian houses that dominate the buildings throughout the town, and the different levels of land as the houses, cottages and commercial buildings steadily rise on the hillsides capped at the summit by The Crescent. We could visualize the werewolf chasing people through that town during the full moon but never settled down enough to write the book. Life got in the way as it often does, and we were too busy with other projects.

The views from the summit of Jerome were spectacular as were those from the west side of Eureka Springs looking to East Mountain. Jerome's wide, colorful valley with the natural monumental red rock formations in the distance rivaled Eureka Springs' gigantic lit up statue of Jesus with his hands outstretched on East Mountain.

That first night in Eureka Springs when we saw the humongous monstrosity which is really a marker for a tomb where an influential man and his wife are buried, Kel left a note in the guest book of the cottage where we stayed that read, " Now I know what Jesus did during the forty days he spent wandering in the wilderness. He stayed lit!"

So proud of what he wrote even though it was a bit sacrilegious, he read it aloud to me and we both laughed. Although the statue was constructed by design, it had a spiritual feeling and

238

meaning to Christians who flocked there to see the Passion Play performances staged during the height of the tourist season.

The large valley to the east of Jerome in all its natural beauty had more of a spiritual feeling to us as we stopped to fill our souls gazing from way above the main area of the little municipality's business section. The two communities were so much alike that we felt as if we were in the Twilight Zone - not quite in Eureka Springs or Jerome but in a weird combination of the two hamlets. We experienced deja vu but we'd certainly never been here before.

Delighted to explore around all over the place we hadn't been there very long when an aroma coming from one of the local eateries wafted into our noses.

"What's that wonderful smell?" I asked Kel at about the same time he was going to ask me that same question.

Letting our noses lead the way we found the Red Rooster Cafe where we looked at their menu to see what was simmering on the stove. The young, earthy woman behind the counter said it was vegetarian potato soup. Unable to resist we each ordered a bowl and sat out front on their porch at one of the small wooden tables to eat it along with the freshly baked whole grain bread that came with it. The soup tasted as good as it smelled, and the bread was hearty and nourishing as well. All too soon we had toured the entire business district and as it was late in the afternoon needed to get back to the girls.

"I'm feeling guilty about not being back to feed the girls on time," I said.

"They'll survive even if they don't get fed right on time," Kel assured me, smiling at my preoccupation with time and schedules even while on vacation.

Of course, the girls were very anxious to get their supper once we arrived back at our cottage. They greeted us as always with vigorous tail wagging and hopping around at our feet while we petted their smooth heads and spoke lovingly to them. I filled their food dishes quickly and after Bea's perfunctory barking they made quick work of their supper.

Since Kel and I'd had our soup and bread snack we weren't hungry for any dinner. Rather than just stay at the cabin we decided to drive over to Doe Mountain, which is really a mesa, to watch the sun go down.

Kel loved to take sunset photos always hoping to capture the rays at just the perfect time when they spread out like giant wagon spokes in a half wheel on the horizon line with the deep reds and oranges glowing against the darkening sky. Once again, the literature Kel had picked up came through with a description of an optimum place to hike and film the sunset. Not included in the brochure though was how creepy Doe Mountain could get.

The sun was still relatively high when we began our ascent of the mesa following the switchbacks upward and around. We were the only humans out there. With my bad right hip, I couldn't walk at a very rapid pace so we couldn't cover much ground as quickly as we wanted to. Climbing upward or downward always inflamed my hip making the pain much worse. Kel could tell when I was hurting by my limp becoming more pronounced as I tried to compensate to get over the throbbing that usually would run all the way down to my right knee. Nevertheless, I wanted to do the climb and never let my bad hip stop me from whatever I wanted to attempt.

240

We went up and around up and around and up and around some more for what seemed like a very long time. I was beginning to wonder if there was ever going to be a flattened plateau area to this mesa. The sun was beginning to set now and Kel was in a panic to make it all the way to the top before it completely disappeared since he wanted to get at least one or two photos. My slower gait was holding him back, but he didn't want to run off and leave me. I knew how Bea must feel whenever B.B. always outruns her. Finally, we were at the end of our climb where Kel furiously snapped as many sunset photos as he could while we gazed across towards the mountain in the distance to the west. Named Bear Mountain, the sun was rapidly heading downward behind it.

Since Old Sol had treated us to his spectacular last hurrah before disappearing it had been worth the effort and pain.

It wasn't long until Kel said, "We better start down. I read that there are mountain lions in this part of the desert. They come out at dusk to hunt so we better get down as quickly as we can. I don't want us to become dinner for one of them."

"Oh, you're just saying that to scare me," I accused him knowing what a joker he always is and how he sometimes gets a kick out of scaring me.

"I'm not kidding. There really ARE mountain lions up in this place and we really DO need to scale down this mountain in record time. We sure don't want to be caught out here without a light when it gets pitch black."

Now I realized in horror that he wasn't pulling my leg. This was the first time he'd mentioned anything about predators in the area and immediately becoming alarmed, my imagination began to conjure up images of giant mountain lions silently stalking us with the darkness closing in while we tried in vain to get down off the mountain before they sprang upon us. Hip or no bad hip I hurried along as I looked fearfully over my shoulder upon hearing the breaking of a twig or any small sound. The birds had stopped singing having found a safe place to roost for the night. Kel even acted spooked out which again confirmed that he wasn't faking it for my benefit. It seemed even longer going down and around the switchbacks than it had climbing up due to the fear and dread of being attacked by a wild animal.

" I can't believe I came out here without even a light to guide our path. And I didn't even bring my mace," Kel scolded himself as we kept swiftly moving around the switchbacks.

"We've just got to hurry up and get to the car," I whispered, afraid I might alert a mountain lion to our location if I spoke too loudly. "How much farther do you think it is?"

"I don't know. There's nothing really to landmark on now that it's getting so dark," Kel answered back softly.

Our footsteps on the rocky pathway were the only sounds I heard but having seen many nature films I knew that big cats can move without making any sound at all when stalking their prey. With my imagination running wild how I wished we'd brought our lantern that we always packed in the car on these dog vacations. We both carry small mace canisters in our bicycle packs just in case we come in contact with a vicious dog or person while riding. Now that we really might needed them, of course, we'd left them with our bicycles for safekeeping. As we

242

moved down the mountain at as fast a pace as possible without falling we both had the eerie sensation of being watched by some silent predator and at every turn I was sure there would be eyes in the darkness that belonged to a huge creature just waiting to spring on us.

I even began to think of werewolves too since my memory about the book we'd dreamed of writing had been sparked in Jerome. That thought didn't bother me nearly as much as the reality that there could be a real live mountain lion or bear on our trail or lying in wait for the right moment to pounce. It spurred me to get along even faster glad that it was downhill. That feeling of being followed wouldn't go away as it was lodged in my brain worrying me all the way down.

Finally, as inky blackness descended on Doe Mountain, we reached the end of our descent and hurried through the stretch of desert to the car. I couldn't limp quickly enough to get there. We'd barely gotten down before it became too dark to see our surroundings. Grabbing my keys from the pocket of my jeans I hastily unlocked it so we could escape the grasp of danger which I felt had been tightening its prickly fingers around us. Thankful for the safety of the car I locked the doors behind us and started her up.

"I'm so relieved to be back in the car and getting out of here!" I expressed my emotions to Kel, who was just as glad to be okay and leaving too.

"Yeah, I just wish I would've remembered some necessary items as a precaution," he said, ruefully. "I was trained as a Boy Scout better than that."

"Well, all's well that ends well. I don't know what we'd have done if we had seen a mountain lion," I said, my eyes growing big again with that fearful thought.

"I've heard that you have to make yourself look large and scary then pick up a stick or a rock or something to use as a defensive weapon. Or at least make it think you did and keep eye contact. What you must NOT do is run since that'll just cause the attacker to give chase."

"Well, I'm just glad we didn't have to defend ourselves. We'll be back to the girls soon. It would've been terrible if we'd have been hurt or killed and the girls would be left all alone," I speculated.

"Let's not worry about it anymore. We're safe and that's what counts."

It was an even more joyous reunion with Bea and B.B. back at the cottage. If I'd have had a tail, I would've wagged it as uproariously as they wagged theirs upon seeing us walk through the sliding door.

We'd had enough of going out for that night, so we pulled some health food out of the refrigerator and made a meal on that for our supper when we heated it up in the microwave. After all we'd eaten quite a lot of food during the whole day, so we weren't terribly hungry. Our little car refrigerator wouldn't hold as much food as we had left over so we needed to consume some anyway. I was never one to waste food if I could help it. This was our last night here in The Tree House as we'd depart tomorrow morning. Extremely relieved that it hadn't been our last night on earth we sat on the balcony enjoying the pleasant weather even more as we reviewed the day's activities. It had been another fun and exciting day chocked full of adventure, some of it more than we bargained for. As tired as I was, I knew falling asleep would be easy. The girls curled around our feet comfortingly as we sat on the balcony for the last time before we all trudged in to go to bed.

Chapter 4   The Road Home

The end of May just happened to coincide with the end of our trip. Since I hadn't felt like doing anything but sitting out on the balcony for a while before bed to try and recover from our scare at Doe Mountain, I had to pack up all our stuff this morning.

Taking the girls on a last walk down the nearby trail was the first order of business.   The sun was up, and the birds were chirping as we moved down the path taking in all the sights, smells, and sounds for the final time. The girls had had lots of fun and adventures which always makes me happy when I see how genuinely they enjoy themselves. Dogs never fake pleasure - they wear their emotions right out on their darling faces for the whole world to see making it quite easy to tell if they're truly having fun. They're totally transparent unlike people who more-often-than-not hide their true feelings.

"We'll need to get an early start since we're going to lose an hour when we hit the New Mexico state line," I pled my case. "It's going to be a long drive over 500 miles, so we really need to get going as soon as possible."

I emphasized this point to my dear man who hardly ever got concerned about linear time while he lingered over his coffee in bed with the girls vying for his attention. By some amazing quirk of fate, we were able to get on the road early that morning as we bid a fond farewell to Sedona and The Forest Houses Resort.

" I think we'll be back here someday," Kel said as we started to drive up and out of the place.

"I sure hope so. This is such a fun place with so many interesting things to do."

It rained lightly on us once we crossed into New Mexico and pulled into the same Motel 6 which now seemed like a home away from home. Tucumcari was beginning to feel like an old friend as it was so easy and comfortable to be back there. The girls even seemed to recognize where they were. After walking around in the area so Bea and B.B. could do their business which I cleaned up I tried to feed them but neither one of them acted the least bit hungry. Bea went straight to her bed and curled up as Kel turned on the TV so we could go eat at Del's Mexican Restaurant. Their lack of appetite had us concerned but we didn't know what we should do about it.

"I just hope they'll be ready to eat later."

"They must be exhausted from the long drive," Kel observed.

Our appetites were a different matter so that by the time we were able to go eat after the unpacking, walking the girls, and putting out their food, we were famished. The hour was getting late but since it was a Friday night, we figured the restaurant would still be open.

Business was booming and we had to wait for a table. It seemed like everyone in town had decided to eat at the popular place once the work week had ended. I remembered how my parents and I had always gone to eat at Brook's Fine Foods in Bartlesville every Friday night when I was in grade school so long ago.

When I was just in the first grade, we began doing that and continued all the way through my years in elementary school. The routine was as regular as a ticking metronome. I had my piano lesson with Mrs. Nellie McReady Wilson at her studio that was adjacent to her house in town.

She always bolstered me by saying, "I'm going to make a concert pianist out of you," recognizing my extraordinary talent for music since playing the piano came very easily to me. Ever since I could remember I loved music. An extraordinarily gifted music teacher, I think she might've accomplished the goal she set out for me had she not passed away when I was just beginning the third grade.

After my lesson I was given seventy-five cents allowance before we went for supper at Brook's where I always ordered tenderloin of trout. Our Friday night routine changed a little when she died. My allowance went up steadily over the years and my piano lessons were moved to Saturday mornings for a while. The only thing that didn't change was eating at Brook's on Friday nights although I switched to ordering hamburger steaks. Funny how the ordinary pleasures remain so firmly in the memory and become more important as you age.

Eating at Del's that Friday night caused a wave of nostalgia to wash over me as I thought about my parents and those happy long-gone days. Typical since once again we were on the road home.

The sky let loose with a cloudburst preceded by a huge crack of thunder just as we finished our meal. I worried about the girls and how frightened they would be, especially B.B. It was pouring as we hurried to the car. But we wouldn't melt and needed to get back to the girls to try and calm them in case they had heard the thunder.

The channel was on "American Idol," a show we were following from the beginning this year

247

since native Oklahoman Carrie Underwood from Checotah was climbing the ranks throughout the season. We were rooting for her to win it all with her tremendous voice and her ability to sing pretty much any style of music with such a strong, clear, beautiful tone. The fact that she's a vegetarian too and cares deeply for animals of all species, not just dogs and cats, made us like her even more. Since we went out to eat during the time it was airing, we missed most of the final show. They were interviewing her because she'd won the whole ball of vinyl! It thrilled us that she was assured to have a great career now that she was "discovered." As Simon Cowell put it, he believed she'd "sell more CDs and be more successful than any other contestant that had ever won the title." I couldn't have agreed more. Anyone who watches TV or follows country music at all knows that his prediction came to pass. Following her meteoric rise to fame and all her awards and accomplishments over the many years, it doesn't seem like it will end any time soon. Kel and I discussed many times about how she looks even better than when she first hit the stage on American Idol. Perfect from the beginning, we don't think she could ever improve on her singing. She certainly is an American idol and as native Oklahomans we're very proud of the excellent representative she is for our state.

The next morning after I took the girls for their walk around the motel property even Bea refused to eat her food again. I was used to B.B. not wanting to touch hers at times since she had a flighty stomach, but Miss Bea nearly always wolfed hers down after the barking ritual aimed at B.B. Their refusal to eat again worried me. Out early for our morning walk, they did their normal business. Thinking that B.B. might need to eat grass to make herself throw up I decided

248

to walk them again. Purging herself was a rather common occurrence about twice a week when we were at home. But this time she didn't eat any grass and there wasn't' much grass to eat in this desert anyway. They neither one did much else except sniff around a little so giving up I took them back inside thinking that after we ate our breakfast down at the good old standby Route 66 diner, we'd bring them back some bacon that we wouldn't eat but which came with the meals. Once I placed it on their dry dog food surely that would get them to eat.

The bacon did the trick as they smelled it when we first stepped into the room, and then were all over Kel wiggling around his legs begging for some of it as their tails lashed the air around them. He quickly put a piece on each ration of food that was still sitting untouched. They ate lustily now and licked their bowls. I was so relieved seeing them gobble it all down. Thank goodness for that bacon! We try to never let it pass our lips but it sure saved the day for our spoiled girls.

It would be another long drive to get back but not as far as the one the day before. We'd lose another hour when we crossed into Texas. We knew the highway quite well since we'd been down it so many times with all its gaudy signs advertising among other things the Big Texan Steakhouse in Amarillo where if you could finish off some ungodly seventy-two ounces of steak and all the trimmings, you'd get your meal for free. I wondered how many people had been able to eat that much food. Photos were displayed on the walls of everyone who'd accomplished that rather dubious feat. In my opinion it wasn't anything to be proud of. Gluttony, one of the seven deadly sins, was alive and well. There were tourist traps all along the way which we didn't ever stop in to look at the trinkets they were offering much less buy any of it. I couldn't believe that people would frequent those places, but they obviously had business, or they wouldn't have been surviving still. Eating at a rest area out in a natural setting while the girls entertained us by just doing what came naturally was way more preferable to us.

Now we cleaned up and packed the few things we'd unpacked the night before then hit the road for home at a reasonably early time. It was a beautiful day to travel. The rain had ended, and the sun was spreading its warm rays embracing everything it touched as we finished loading up the car and called the girls to speed out of the room and leap into the waiting backseat. So with the Little Handle-less Refrigerator That Could humming away behind my seat in its spot on the floor, the bicycles securely strapped into the bike rack, everything else put in its proper place, and the girls standing in the back seat too excited to settle down yet, I pointed the car east on I-40 as we left dusty Tucumcari behind in the rearview mirror.

There was much barking and carrying on at the cows and "horsiecows" in the fields all along the way. Arriving at our home sweet home by late afternoon after a very smooth and easy trip we were all glad that everything looked just perfect there. The girls were as happy as we to be back home. They ran to the sliding door and asked with their eyes to be let into their fenced backyard after they sniffed around through the house. B.B. looked to see if there were any squirrels up in the tall trees. We hastily unpacked the car starting with the bicycles and the refrigerator before bringing in all the rest of the bags and other articles in the proper order. Once we got everything piled into the foyer on the floor, we took the girls for a short walk before I fed them their supper. They marked their territory the entire time while we were walking. It'd been a week since they'd left their scent on it. Other neighborhood dogs had covered over it so B.B., especially was anxious to make sure everyone knew she was back.

As we came walking up our sidewalk by the little flowers in pots, I noticed that one plant that doesn't drain well had water standing in its container. That meant we must've had some rain. The pond across the street looking so fat and full also confirmed that. The grass and bushes were bright green and lush. It felt nice to be back in our bucolic neighborhood again after such a fun-filled trip. No matter how far we traveled or what lovely sights we saw I always regarded our neighborhood as the most beautiful place on earth.

I was so beat from rising at the crack of dawn and driving that I went to bed before a movie we were watching concluded. It didn't really matter as I'd seen it before. It felt good to sink into the comfort of my own bed up in our lovely master bedroom after tucking our girls into their beds on the floor.

"Night, night sleep tight, don't let the bedbugs bite, and I'll see you in the morning bright," I whispered to each of them as I kissed their smooth heads smiling to myself at how lucky I am to have such a good life with Kel and the Bestest Dogs in the Whole Wide World!